BLAKE'S

Science Guide

for primary students

Donna Bennett

PASCAL PRESS

Blake's Science Guide

ISBN: 978 1742 159027

Published by Pascal Press
PO Box 250
Glebe NSW 2037
www.pascalpress.com.au
contact@pascalpress.com.au

Author: Donna Bennett
Publisher: Lynn Dickinson
Edited by Karen Jayne
Design and illustration by Janice Bowles

CONTENTS

How to use this book 4
Quick guide to topics 5
Introduction 6
Australian curriculum correlations 7

SCIENCE INQUIRY SKILLS 11
Scientific investigation 11
Questioning and predicting 12
Senses 12
Is observing seeing? 12
Measuring 13
Hypothesis – getting the guess right 14
Literature search 14
Recipe for a hypothesis 15
Hypothesis formulation 15
Predictions from a hypothesis 17
Planning an investigation 18
What is a variable? 18
Types of variables 19
Designing investigations 20
Checklist for experimental design 20
Characteristics of good experimental design 21
Scientist's tools 23
Laboratory apparatus 23
Measuring tools 24
Measuring and recording data 25
Units of measurement 25
Recording measurements 25
Processing and analysing data 26
Data handling skills 26
Graphing 27
Discrete and continuous data 27
Appropriate graph format 28
Rules for drawing a line graph 30
Evaluation 32
Data analysis and evaluation 32
Checklist for evaluating evidence 33
Conclusion 35
Communicating 37
Writing a report in the scientific format 37
Checklist for report writing 38

BIOLOGICAL SCIENCES 39
Biology – the study of life 39
The condition of being alive 39
Cells: the basic unit of life 40
The chemistry of life 41
Classification of life 42
Plant kingdom 45
Plant groups 45
Plant structure 46
Plant processes 47
Plant growth 48
Plant reproduction 49
Animal kingdom 50
Animal groups 50
Animal systems 52
Animal processes 53
Animal growth 53
Animal feeding 54
Animal movement 56
Animal senses 56
Animal communication 57
Animal behaviour 58
Animal reproduction 59
Ecology 61
Environment 61

CONTENTS continued...

Flow of energy and matter in the natural world 63
Survival and the interaction of living things 66
Ecosystem balance 67

PHYSICAL SCIENCES 70

Energy 70
What is energy? 70
Where do we get energy from? 70
How does energy behave? 71
Forms of energy 72
Potential energy 72
Kinetic energy 73
Heat energy 74
What does 'hot' and 'cold' mean? 74
Heat transfer 74
Conductors and insulators 75
Controlling heat transfer 76
Expansion and contraction 76
Light energy 77
What is light? 77
What colour is light? 78
Sensing light 79
Reflection – bouncing light 79
Refraction – bending light 80
How we use light 81
Sound energy 83
What is sound? 83
Sensing sound 84
How sound travels 84
Musical sounds 85
Sound and our world 86
Electrical energy 88
Types of electricity 88
Building circuits 89
Force 91
Balanced and unbalanced forces 91
Contact forces 92
Non-contact forces 94
Motion 97
Newton's first law of motion 97
Newton's second law of motion 98
Newton's third law of motion 99

CHEMICAL SCIENCES 100

What are materials? 100
What is matter? 100
Characteristics of matter 101
Classifying materials 102
Mixtures 102
Pure substances 103
The 'states of matter' 104
Solids, liquids and gases 104
Combining the states of matter 106
Changing materials 107
Physical change 107
Chemical change 108
Properties of materials 109
Natural materials 109
Processed materials 110
Choosing and using materials 111
Strength of materials 111
Piles and piles of garbage 113
Processing garbage 113
Biodegradable materials 114
Recycling materials 114
Recycling plastics 115

CONTENTS continued...

EARTH & SPACE SCIENCES	**117**
Time	**117**
Keeping track of time	117
Geological time	118
Planet Earth	**119**
The Earth in space	119
Dimensions of time and scale	119
Third rock from the Sun	121
Earth's rotations	121
The Moon	123
Structure of the Earth	**125**
Changing landscapes	126
Earth's soils	126
Geo-superstars	129
Weather	**133**
Atmosphere and weather	133
Water and weather	135
Oceans and weather	136
Climate and weather	136
Earth's resources and human activity	**139**
Atmosphere and life	139
Water and life	141
Soils and life	142
HUMAN ENDEAVOUR	**144**
What is science?	**144**
Limits of science	144
Research	144
Scientific view	**145**
Key aspects	145
Levels of scientific thought	146
Scientific literacy	147
Scientific numeracy	148
Science involves problem solving	**149**
Science tips for solving problems	149
What do scientists do?	**150**
Observation	150
Visualise	150
Field research	151
Study systems	152
Compare things	152
Name things	153
Test ideas	153
Collaborate	153
Communicate	154
Use technology	155
Make decisions	155
The qualities of a scientist	**156**
Creativity	156
Honesty and integrity	156
Scepticism	156
Imagination	157
Ethics	157
Wisdom	158
Science in society	**159**
Intercultural understanding	159
Current issues	159
Glossary	160
'Try This' Answers	165
Index	171

HOW TO USE THIS BOOK

Blake's Science Guide provides you with the tools you need to be successful with science investigations. It will help you develop knowledge and understanding about scientific method and how this method can be applied to test ideas relating to the natural world.

This guide contains:

- sections on each key aspect of the Australian primary science curriculum
- examples for each new concept
- opportunities to practise science investigation with the TRY THIS sections
- guidelines for developing and testing hypothesis for scientific ideas
- ideas on how science can provide a reliable base for making decisions, generalising and making predictions
- a comprehensive glossary for all major terms
- a detailed index for locating specific terms
- answers to the TRY THIS sections.

Blake's Science Guide is a vital reference for the study of scientific method and how science relates to the world around us.

ABOUT THE AUTHOR

Donna Bennett is a highly qualified and experienced teacher. She is the winner of two national awards, the CRA Mining Company Fellowship and the BHP Science Teacher Award for innovative and creative delivery of science. She is the Director of Science Education Australia and her science workshop programs are always popular with teachers and students. Donna has written several successful science education books, established a Queensland Science Marathon and has taken her 'Science for Bush Kids' program to regional areas.

QUICK GUIDE to TOPICS

This table provides a quick page reference to popular topics within and between science strands. Use this table in conjunction with the index and contents pages.

TOPIC	Science Inquiry Skills	Biological Sciences	Physical Sciences	Chemical Sciences	Earth & Space Science	Human Endeavour
Animals	29, 31	42–44, 50–60				151–152
Change	20	39, 47–48, 52–54, 59–60, 67		107–108	117–118, 126–127	146
Earth in Space			94–95		119–124	144
Energy	26	63–66	70–90		129–132, 134, 136	
Environment	21	61–62, 68–69	86–87	113–116	125–132, 139–143	152
Forces			91–96, 97–99		121, 131, 136	
Materials	18–19, 34		76	102–103, 109–112		
Matter			72–73	100–116	126–129	
Micro-organisms		39–41				146
Movement		46, 56			130–132, 134–138	
Plants		45–49				151
Senses	12, 14	56	79, 83, 84			150
Water		47			132, 135–138, 141–142	
Weather			133–138			15–16

INTRODUCTION

Why is science so important?

Science is a powerful way of seeking to understand things because it is based on evidence. It allows us to generalise and to make predictions. Science tells us what can be done but we have to also consider what ought to be done.

The importance of science lies in trying to apply the knowledge of science and how the Earth works accurately to everyday decisions. We need to train experts to help manage the interaction of humans with the planet. The work of scientists reflects the nature and development of science. Scientist's work is built around scientific inquiry and seeks to respond and to influence society's needs. Every person needs to have some knowledge of the issues involved in living in Australia and the world.

The game of science is about curiosity that turns into the satisfaction of knowledge. It should begin with some fun and end with wisdom.

Science is not about a set of procedures or ideas that students are supposed to follow mindlessly. It is not a bunch of 'facts' to be accepted and not challenged. It is not about using a format to produce a desired outcome.

Science raises confronting questions and develops the ability to make informed decisions about global and 'backyard' issues. This guide separates science from myth. It separates considered opinion from hasty judgement. It guides students to realise that of all the things that are scientifically possible, not all are desirable.

In this guide, the three strands in the curriculum – Science Understanding, Science as a Human Endeavour and Science Inquiry Skills are closely integrated. The Australian Curriculum advises that science should be taught in an integrated way.

Overarching ideas in science

There are basic notions in science that represent key aspects of a scientific view of the world and bridge knowledge and understanding across the disciplines of science.

We should understand that:

- Physics is the same everywhere in the universe. For example, the speed of light is constant no matter where you are or what you are doing.
- The Universe and everything in the Universe is made up of only three things – energy, atoms and the spaces in between the atoms.
- All matter is made up of particles called atoms (elements), which are too small to see. Atoms organise themselves according to rules and regulations that scientists are still discovering. On Earth, we are far enough away from the Sun's energy so that matter can be in one or more of the following states – solid, liquid and gas.
- No one really knows what energy is, but we do know that nothing at all can happen in the Universe without energy.

AUSTRALIAN CURRICULUM CORRELATIONS - YEAR 3

SCIENCE INQUIRY SKILLS	ELABORATIONS	ACSIS	PAGE
Questioning and predicting			
With guidance, identify questions in familiar contexts that can be investigated scientifically and predict what might happen based on prior knowledge	★ considering familiar situations in order to think of possible areas for investigation	53	13, 15
Planning and conducting			
Suggest ways to plan and conduct investigations to find answers to questions	★ test simple cause-and-effect relationships	54	18–21
Safely use appropriate materials, tools or equipment to make and record observations, using formal measurements and digital technologies as appropriate	★ recording measurements using familiar formal units and appropriate abbreviations	55	23–25
Processing and analysing data and information			
Use a range of methods including tables and simple column graphs to represent data and to identify patterns and trends	★ using tables to organise materials and objects based on observable properties ★ identifying and discussing numerical and visual patterns in data	57	28–29, 31
Compare results with predictions, suggesting possible reasons for findings	★ discussing how well predictions matched results from an investigation and sharing ideas about what was learnt	215	35–36
Evaluating			
Reflect on the investigation, including whether a test was fair or not	★ describing experiences of carrying out investigations	58	33–34
Communicating			
Represent and communicate ideas and findings in a variety of ways such as diagrams, physical representations and simple reports	★ using simple explanations and arguments, reports or graphical representations to communicate ideas to other students	60	37–38
SCIENCE UNDERSTANDING		**ACSSU**	
Biological sciences			
Living things can be grouped on the basis of observable features and can be distinguished from non-living things	★ exploring differences between living, once living and products of living things	44	39, 42–51 54
	★ sorting living things based on characteristics		57–60
	★ recognising characteristics and the range of living things		65–66
Chemical sciences			
A change of state between solid and liquid can be caused by adding or removing heat	★ investigating how liquids and solids respond to changes in temperature	46	107
Earth and space sciences			117
Earth's rotation on axis causes regular changes, including day and night	★ describing timescales for the rotation of the Earth	48	122
Physical sciences			
Heat can be produced in many ways and can move from one object to another	★ describing how heat can be produced through friction or motion ★ identifying changes that occur in everyday situations due to heating and cooling ★ exploring how heat can be transferred through conduction	49	74–76
SCIENCE AS A HUMAN ENDEAVOUR		**ACSHE**	
Nature and development of science			
Science involves making predictions and describing patterns and relationships	★ making predictions about change and events in our environment and considering how posing questions helps us plan for the future	50	147–48

AUSTRALIAN CURRICULUM CORRELATIONS - YEAR 4

SCIENCE INQUIRY SKILLS	ELABORATIONS	ACSIS	PAGE
Questioning and predicting With guidance, identify questions in familiar contexts that can be investigated scientifically and predict what might happen based on prior knowledge	★ considering familiar situations in order to think of possible areas for investigation	64	13, 15
Planning and conducting Suggest ways to plan and conduct investigations to find answers to questions	★ to test simple cause-and-effect relationships	65	18–21
Safely use appropriate materials, tools or equipment to make and record observations, using formal measurements and digital technologies as appropriate	★ recording measurements using formal units	66	23–25
Processing and analysing data and information Use a range of methods including tables and simple column graphs to represent data and to identify patterns and trends	★ using tables to organise materials based on observations ★ identifying and discussing numerical and visual patterns in data collected	68	28–29, 31
Compare results with predictions, suggesting possible reasons for findings	★ discussing how well predictions matched results from an investigation	216	35–36
Evaluating Reflect on investigations, including including whether a test was fair or not	★ describing experiences of carrying out investigations	69	33–34
Communicating Represent and communicate ideas and findings in a variety of ways such as diagrams, physical representations and simple reports	★ using simple explanations and arguments, reports or graphical representations to communicate ideas	71	37–38
SCIENCE UNDERSTANDING		**ACSSU**	
Biological sciences Living things have life cycles	★ describing the stages of life cycles ★ recognising that environmental factors can affect life cycles such as fire and seed germination	72	48, 54
Living things, including plants and animals, depend on each other and the environment to survive	★ predicting the effects when living things in feeding relationships are removed or die out in an area ★ investigating the roles of living things in a habitat ★ recognising that interactions between living things may be competitive or mutually beneficial	73	62, 64–66
Chemical sciences Natural and processed materials have a range of physical properties; these properties can influence their use	★ considering how the properties of materials affect the management of waste or can lead to pollution ★ describing some common materials and their uses	74	100 109–16
Earth and space sciences Earth's surface changes over time as a result of natural processes and human activity	★ considering how different human activities cause erosion and other events on the landscape ★ investigating the characteristics of soils	75	126–27 136–38 142–43
Physical sciences Forces can be exerted by one object on another through direct contact or from a distance	★ comparing the effect of friction between different surfaces and investigating the forces of attraction and repulsion between magnets	76	92–96
SCIENCE AS A HUMAN ENDEAVOUR		**ACSHE**	
Nature and development of science Science involves making predictions and describing patterns and relationships	★ exploring ways in which scientists gather evidence for their ideas and develop explanations	61	150–55
Use and influence of science Science knowledge helps people to understand the effect of their actions	★ exploring how science has contributed to a discussion about an issue such as loss of habitat	62	159

AUSTRALIAN CURRICULUM CORRELATIONS - YEAR 5

SCIENCE INQUIRY SKILLS	ELABORATIONS	ACSIS	PAGE
Questioning and predicting With guidance, pose questions to clarify practical problems or inform a scientific investigation, and predict what the findings of an investigation might be	★ applying experience from similar situations in the past to make predictions in a new situation	231	15–16
Planning and conducting With guidance, select appropriate investigation methods to answer questions or solve problems	★ considering different investigation methods such as experimental testing	86	11, 18, 20–22
Decide which variable should be changed and measured in fair tests and accurately observe, measure and record data using digital technologies as appropriate	★ using the ideas of an independent variable as something that is being investigated by changing it and measuring the effect of this change ★ using familiar tools to measure objects and events	87	18–19, 23
Processing and analysing data and information Construct and use a range of representations, including tables and graphs, to represent and describe observations, patterns or relationships in data using digital technologies as appropriate	★ identifying similarities and differences in qualitative data in order to group items or materials ★ describing simple cause-and-effect relationships as shown by trends in quantitative data	90	29, 31
Evaluating Suggest improvements to the methods used to investigate a question or solve a problem	★ working collaboratively to suggest improvements to the methods used	91	33–34
Communicating Communicate ideas, explanations and processes in a variety of ways, including multi-modal texts	★ using a variety of communication models to communicate scientific ideas	93	37–38
SCIENCE UNDERSTANDING		**ACSSU**	
Biological sciences Living things have structural features and adaptations that help them survive in their environment	★ exploring general adaptations for particular environments such as water conservation in deserts ★ describing and listing adaptations of living things suited for the Australian environment ★ explaining how particular adaptations help survival ★ comparing types of adaptations	43	67
Chemical sciences Solids, liquids and gases have different observable properties and behave in different ways	★ exploring the ways solids, liquids and gases change under different situations ★ recognising that some materials are composite materials and cannot be easily classified as solids, liquids or gases based on observable properties	77	104–08
Earth and space sciences The Earth is part of a system of planets orbiting around a star (the sun)	★ modelling the relative size of and distance between Earth, other planets in the solar system and the sun	78	119–20
Physical sciences Light from a source forms shadows and can be absorbed, reflected and refracted	★ classifying materials as transparent, opaque or translucent based on the effect of light ★ recognising that colour depends on the properties of the object and the colour of the light source ★ exploring the use of mirrors to demonstrate the reflection of light ★ recognising the refraction of light at the surfaces of different transparent materials	80	79–81

AUSTRALIAN CURRICULUM CORRELATIONS - YEAR 6

SCIENCE INQUIRY SKILLS	ELABORATIONS	ACSIS	PAGE
Questioning and predicting			
With guidance, pose questions to clarify practical problems or inform a scientific investigation, and predict what the findings of an investigation might be	★ applying experience from similar situations in the past to make predictions in a new situation	232	15–16
Planning and conducting			
With guidance, select appropriate investigation methods to answer questions or solve problems	★ considering different investigation methods such as experimental testing	103	11, 18, 20–22
Decide which variable should be changed and measured in fair tests and accurately observe, measure and record data, using digital technologies as appropriate	★ using the ideas of an independent variable as something that is being investigated by changing it and measuring the effect of this change ★ using familiar tools to measure objects and events	104	18–19
Processing and analysing data and information			
Construct and use a range of representations, including tables and graphs, to represent and describe observations, patterns or relationships in data using digital technologies as appropriate	★ identifying similarities and differences in qualitative data in order to group items or materials ★ describing simple cause-and-effect relationships as shown by trends in quantitative data	107	29, 31
Evaluating			
Suggest improvements to the methods used to investigate a question or solve a problem	★ working collaboratively to suggest improvements to the methods used	108	33–34
Communicating			
Communicate ideas, explanations and processes in a variety of ways, including multi-modal texts	★ using a variety of communication models to communicate scientific ideas	110	37–38
SCIENCE UNDERSTANDING		**ACSSU**	
Biological sciences			
The growth and survival of living things are affected by the physical conditions of their environment	★ investigating how changing the physical conditions for plants impacts on their growth and survival ★ considering the effects of physical conditions causing migration and hibernation	94	47–48
Chemical sciences			
Changes to materials can be reversible, such as melting, freezing, evaporating; or irreversible, such as burning or rusting	★ exploring how reversible changes can be used to recycle materials	95	102–03
	★ investigating irreversible changes		108
	★ describing what happens when materials are mixed		114–16
Earth and space sciences			
Sudden geological changes or extreme weather conditions can affect Earth's surface	★ investigating major geological events in Australia, the Asia region and throughout the world	96	129–32
	★ exploring ways that scientific understanding can assist in natural disaster management to minimise both long- and short-term effects ★ recognising that earthquakes can cause tsunamis ★ considering the effect of drought on living and non-living aspects of the environment		136–38
Physical sciences			
Electrical circuits provide a means of transferring and transforming electricity	★ recognising the need for a complete circuit to allow the flow of electricity ★ exploring the features of electrical devices such as switches and light globes	97	88–90

SCIENCE INQUIRY SKILLS

Science inquiry skills develop knowledge and understanding about the scientific method and how the method can be used as a tool for testing ideas.

The scientific method is a way of asking a question

SCIENTIFIC INVESTIGATION

Science is like a game for understanding the universe. The game is played by special rules called the '**scientific method**'. The scientific method is a great tool to use to find out about science.

The scientific method rules involve:

- asking a question
- gathering information about the question
- forming the hypothesis
- putting the hypothesis to the test
- drawing a conclusion
- telling others about what you found out.

A **scientific investigation** may involve testing in laboratory conditions, fieldwork, conducting surveys or using **models**.

For example, doing a scientific investigation is like being a detective investigating a mystery. The scientific method is used as a plan for organising an investigation. It is a way of asking a question (A bank was robbed. Who is the robber?) and exploring the information to find the answers (looking at the clues). When using the scientific method, scientists must remember that the rules are flexible and are only a general plan.

Anyone who loves science knows that hunches, wrong turns, intuition and the ideas that did not work make scientific discovery the most challenging, exhilarating, frustrating, yet exciting adventure ever devised.

QUESTIONING AND PREDICTING

Observing starts people asking questions about something that interests them. Observing things involves using all of our senses, paying attention, thinking through situations and guessing what might occur. Scientists are always exploring, examining the world, asking questions and wondering about things.

Observing involves using all of our senses

Senses

Our five senses are sight, hearing, smell, touch and taste. Our senses are a 'radar' system that feeds us information about the **environment** around us. Each sense supplies our brain with messages and our brain tells our body how to respond. All this information from our ears, eyes, nose, skin and tongue makes us curious. When scientists are curious, they use their senses to gather information and find answers to questions.

Example

Looking at an ant through a microscope uses sight. Recording the croaks made by selected tree frogs requires hearing.

Try this

Match up each sense with the correct job.

SENSE	JOB
eye	**A** detects chemical substances in the mouth
nose	**B** detects temperature, touch, pain
tongue	**C** detects vibrations in the air
ear	**D** detects light
skin	**E** detects chemicals in the air

Is observing seeing?

Observation is far more than just seeing. Observing means that you work with all your senses as well as your brain to put information together. Our observations can be influenced by many things. What a person sees can depend on what they expect to see.

Example

Different people notice different things when looking at the same scene. Imagine a bushfire. A person running away from the fire, a child watching and a firefighter would all make different observations about the scene.

A student looked at this picture and saw a tree with seedlings growing under it.

1 What do you see?
2 Do you notice anything else about where the seedlings are growing?
3 What further questions might this observation raise?

MEASURING

Accurate measurement is important in science. We can help our sense organs to measure accurately by using instruments and equipment. Measurements also make observations more likely to be understood by other people.

Example

A magnifying glass enhances our ability to see, a thermometer helps us with touch and an amplifier assists hearing ability.

In each case, which of the following observations are more likely to be understood?

A It was a cold day.
The temperature fell to 6 degrees Celsius at 4 pm.

B The band was very noisy.
From the front seat, the sound measured 110 decibels.

HYPOTHESIS – GETTING THE GUESS RIGHT

In science, nothing can be proved – only disproved.

Scientific researchers usually have a guess when trying to explain some natural **phenomenon** that they have observed. However, they always carefully test the guess for accuracy by conducting experiments. Scientists call the guess a **hypothesis**. A hypothesis is a possible explanation for something that has been observed. We should be able to answer yes/no (accepted/unaccepted) to the hypothesis when the experiment has been completed.

Literature search

Before starting work on a problem, scientists do a **literature search** to find out what is already known and recorded. A literature search is used to review available information, or **data**, that supports the proposed research area. Reviewing the available information helps to define what information is missing from the data that is already recorded. It also helps to work out how best to proceed with the investigation.

Example

The following are the steps, in the correct order, for a scientific investigation.

1. *An interesting observation is made by a researcher.*
2. *The researcher asks questions in order to explain the observation.*
3. *A hypothesis or educated guess is devised as the answer.*
4. *An experiment is designed to test the hypothesis.*
5. *An experiment is conducted.*
6. *The hypothesis is rejected or accepted.*

Try this

The scientific investigation is about how our pupils respond to light. Place the following statements into the correct order.

A Question: 'Do the pupils in our eyes respond to light and dark?'
B Hypothesis is accepted.
C Test the reaction of the pupils in a person's eyes to dim light and bright light.
D Hypothesis: 'Dim light will cause the pupils in our eyes to dilate more than bright light.'
E Observe the pupils in a person's eyes dilating.
F Experiment devised to test the dilation of pupils in dim light and bright light.

Recipe for a hypothesis

Combine all the available observations with all the current knowledge about the particular phenomenon or concept. Add a little previous experience, a pinch of intuition, some creative thinking and a flash of inspiration.

A hypothesis or an 'educated guess' must be in a form that is able to be tested to see if it always holds true.

Example

Your own observations tell you that skin often becomes red and sore if exposed to sunlight. Current knowledge tells us that sunlight damages the skin (sunburn) and may cause serious and long lasting problems. This information can be combined with the scientific knowledge that UV radiation causes damage to human skin. Skin cancer has also been linked to UV radiation.

Use the information in the example above to answer the following questions.

1. What does your own intuition tell you about the effects of over exposing your skin to the rays of the sun?
2. Wearing a t-shirt is supposed to reduce sunburn. What question might this information raise?
3. Write a hypothesis that can be tested to answer this question.

Try this

Hypothesis formulation

Forming a hypothesis is one of the most creative parts of scientific investigation. We can use our observations and knowledge to write the hypothesis.

An exceptional hypothesis:

- is based on your observations and knowledge
- is written as a statement, not a question
- contains only one factor that is going to vary.

An exceptional hypothesis should:

- be able to be tested with a simple experiment
- describe the expected results in clear terms.

Example

A viable hypothesis is one that:

- *can be tested*
- *is based on observations*
- *can arrive at one simple answer*
- *is a statement*
- *only contains one variable factor.*

'Sunburn is caused by over exposure to the sun's rays.'
This statement is based on your observational knowledge and is a viable hypothesis.

'The power of UV radiation can be measured using a 'Zeta UV Heliometer.'
This statement is not based on your observational knowledge and is not viable.

'Skin is damaged by over exposure to the weather.'
This hypothesis cannot be tested and is not viable.

'Skin is damaged by over exposure to UV radiation.'
This hypothesis can be tested and is a viable hypothesis.

Try this

Use the information on hypothesis formulation to determine whether the following sentences can be considered a viable hypothesis. For those that are not viable, explain why not.

1 Closely-knit fabrics give better protection than loosely-knit fabrics.

2 Does a sunscreen with a sun protection factor (SPF) of 15 protect better than one with an SPF of 8?

3 Wet fabric gives less protection than dry fabric.

4 Sunscreens work by absorbing UV radiation or by converting it to another form of radiation.

5 Window tinting stops some UV radiation.

6 UV radiation plays a significant role in the development of life on this planet.

7 Polaroid sunglasses reduce the UV radiation reaching our eyes.

Predictions from a hypothesis

A useful hypothesis will help us to make predictions. A prediction is a forecast about a future event. A prediction must be based on a tested and accepted hypothesis.

Sometimes a hypothesis cannot be tested immediately. New discoveries and new technology may be needed to make the necessary experiments feasible.

Example

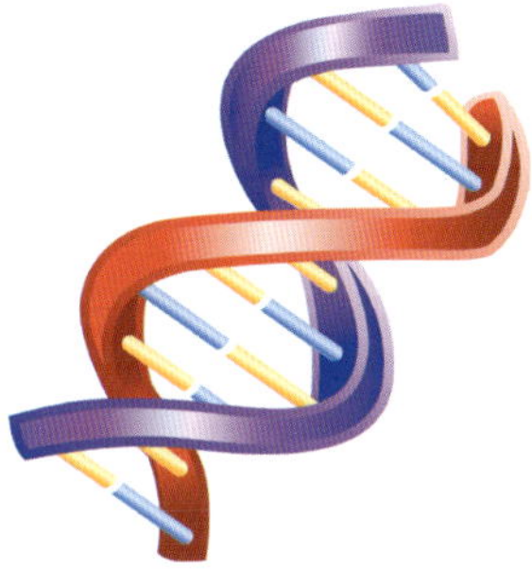

The scientists, Watson and Crick, had guessed that DNA was a twin spiral (double helix), which could 'unzip' to make copies. Years later, using new technology called 'x-ray diffraction imaging' they were able to prove their hypothesis. Watson and Crick went on to predict that it might actually be possible to unravel the DNA codes and copy genetic material. Decades later, scientists are doing just that and much more – genetic engineering.

Once a hypothesis is accepted, then we can begin to make predictions. For example, if we try to turn on a light and nothing happens:

1. What is the problem?
2. What is a reasonable explanation for this observation?
3. What is the best way to test this hypothesis?
4. If your hypothesis is accepted, then what can we now predict?
5. If your hypothesis is not accepted, what must you do?

PLANNING AN INVESTIGATION

An investigation must consider all variables that will affect the situation. To identify correctly the variables, you need to look closely at the hypothesis that you wish to test.

What is a variable?

A **variable** is something that changes in an experiment or in the natural world. For example, temperature and light can change. A **constant** is something that does not change. For example, the force of gravity is a constant because it never changes.

In an experiment, you should choose only one variable to change from one trial to the next. The other variables must be kept the same. The variable you are changing needs to be the important one. When an experiment is repeated, it must produce the same results.

Example

A group of students were curious as to which chocolates have added cocoa butter. Cocoa butter is a yellow fat that is solid at room temperature but melts at body temperature. Manufacturers sometimes add cocoa butter to chocolate to make it seem creamier in the mouth. The variable that is likely to affect this investigation is the temperature of the chocolate.

Try this

The students want to go one step further and see which chocolate they like the taste of best (market research). They selected four different milk chocolates of differing quality – cooking chocolate, inexpensive chocolate, a regular brand and expensive chocolate. They set up a taste test. A good quality chocolate is usually more expensive, melts very fast in your mouth and the flavour should be strong, a little bitter and not too sweet.

1. Which variables did they need to keep constant?
2. Which variable should they change?
3. What other variables, which do not appear to have been considered here, may also be important?
4. This investigation relies on senses that cannot be measured (taste, touch and smell). How could we introduce measurement into this investigation?

Types of variables

A hypothesis proposes a possible cause and effect relationship between two variables. The hypothesis involves the selection of one variable as the cause. It suggests how that variable might affect another variable.

Definitions

- The variable selected as the possible cause is called the **independent variable**. This variable is deliberately altered in some way.
- The variable that changes as a result of the independent variable being altered is called the responding or **dependent variable**.
- There may also be other variables involved but these are kept constant (they do not change) and are called **controlled variables**.

Once we have identified the types of variables and separated them, then it is possible to **design** an experiment so that their individual effects can be studied.

Try this

Example

Main types of variables in the chocolate test

	Independent variable	Dependent variable	Controlled variables
Chocolate investigation	temperature of the chocolate	the presence of cocoa butter	milk chocolate of the same size

The following experiment is about dissolving salt. The variables are dissolving speed, amount of salt, type of salt, water temperature and rate of stirring. Place the variables in the correct columns.

Hypothesis	Independent variable	Dependent variable	Controlled variables
Salt dissolves faster in hot water than in cold.			

DESIGNING INVESTIGATIONS

An experiment is a practical scientific test. Once predictions (hypothesis) have been made and the variables in the hypothesis identified, it is possible to design an experiment to study the possible influence of these variables. Experiments are designed to test the effect of one variable (independent) on another (dependent).

Checklist for experimental design

At the planning stage, you must consider how the hypothesis can be tested.

Do you have the correct resources, equipment and situation to be physically able to conduct the investigation?

Once this has been established then work can proceed. Scientists start designing an investigation by writing a series of steps to be followed (method). The steps outline how the parts of the experiment will be done and in what order.

Example

Students were interested in the biodegradability (how it breaks down) of toilet paper. Research conducted by the students tells them that a biodegradable material can be broken down by natural processes.

The following procedure is a series of steps students followed to test the hypothesis:
'Cheap toilet paper breaks up in water more easily than expensive toilet paper.'

- *Select samples of one cheap and one expensive toilet paper.*
- *Put a sample of each in two different screw cap jars.*
- *Add water to both jars and screw on the lids.*
- *Shake both jars vigorously several times.*
- *Observe how well the paper breaks down.*

In parts of Australia where water is in short supply, irrigation is used to provide additional water to crops. In some places, irrigation has resulted in 'salting' of the soil. Too much salt can have a severe effect on plants.

Hypothesis: 'Soil salinity reduces the germination of lettuce seeds.'

You have the following equipment:

- five pieces of filter paper (to place the seeds on)
- five small containers (four experimental and one control)
- some lettuce seeds (to germinate)
- plastic wrap (to cover the containers so they do not dry out)
- four different salt solutions
- some distilled water.

List the steps that you would take to set up your control and four experimental containers. The control does not have any salt added. Remember that the independent variable should not interfere with the dependent variable.

Clues:

- Do not make **assumptions** or forget things that seem 'obvious'.
- The procedure should be described in detail so that anyone wishing to follow up on your work can see exactly how the data was obtained.
- The list of steps should be in a sensible order.

Characteristics of good experimental design

We plan and organise an experiment so that we learn something. Good experiments do not have to be complicated. A simple hypothesis will give a clear answer (yes or no) when the experiment has been carried out.

Try this

If the experiment produces unexpected results, then the reason should be found.

Experimental validity

For an experiment to be considered 'valid' it must be sound and able to be defended. One way to ensure that an experiment is valid, is to perform the exact same experiment a number of times.

Repeatability

Experiments should be done enough times to be sure that the results are not an accident or a mistake. There should be a large number of tests and results, so that we can be sure that future tests will give the same results. If the results are different, then either the design of the experiment or the way the experiment was performed (or both) is at fault.

Try this

Example

The results of a test, such as the effect of smoking on lung cancer, involving only a few people has not tested enough people. It must be carried out on large numbers of people for the result to be valid.

Losing hair from your head is called 'going bald'. A scientist wanted to find out whether chemical P or chemical Q would cure baldness.

1 Which of the following is the best experimental design? Explain your answer.

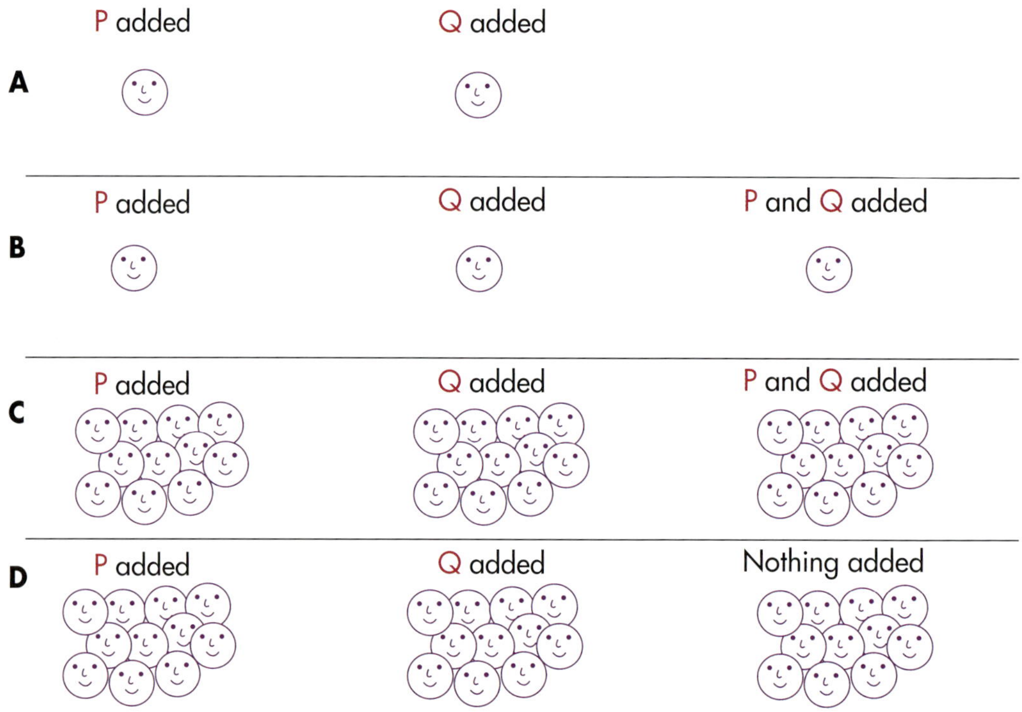

2 Could the chosen design be repeated by other scientists and still get the same results?

3 Could the chosen design be considered experimentally valid? Why?

4 What is the advantage of doing an experiment many times rather than just once?

SCIENTIST'S TOOLS

A laboratory is the place where the work of a scientist is carried out. It is a place, either outdoors or indoors, where scientists ask questions and try to develop answers. Before beginning an experiment, a scientist reads the procedure (method) and gathers all the materials required for each of the steps in the experiment, including the tools or instruments needed to make the measurements.

Laboratory apparatus

Scientists use tools or equipment to make their work easier and measurements more precise. Equipment used in the laboratory is called apparatus. Sometimes very simple apparatus is enough but sometimes sophisticated and complex equipment is needed. There are right and wrong ways to use apparatus. Improper use can lead to mistakes, incorrect results and even disasters.

Choosing instruments

To ensure our observations and the experimental results that we record are accurate, instruments must be chosen carefully.

Example

A ruler is used to measure distance, a stopwatch to measure time, a measuring cylinder to measure volume and an electronic balance to measure weight.

Try this

Accurately read the scales displayed below and record the readings for the ruler, thermometer and measuring cylinder.

1

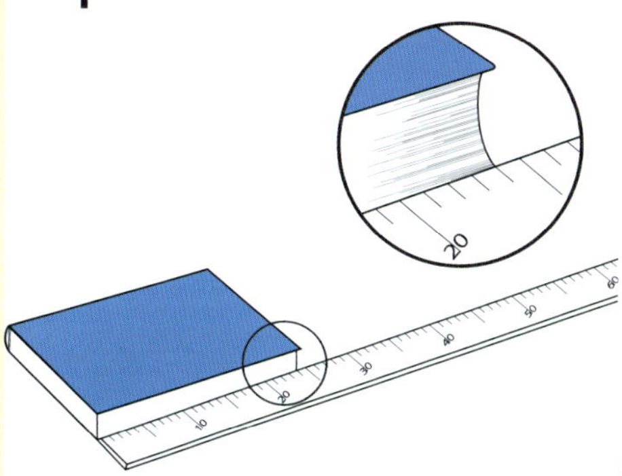

ruler

____

2

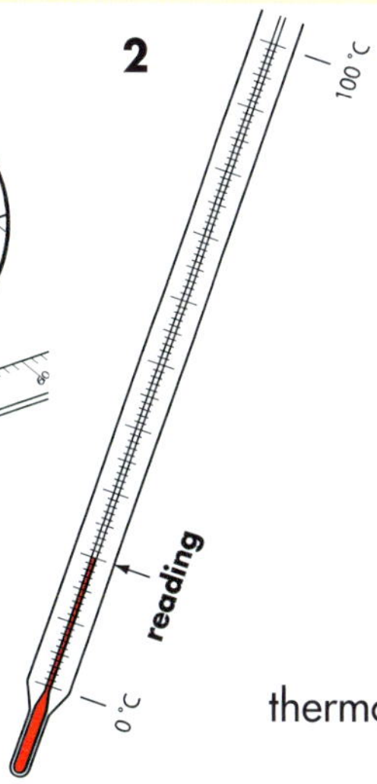

thermometer

____

3

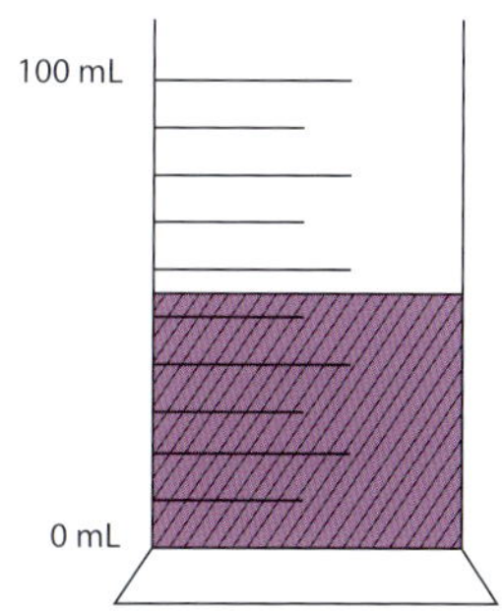

measuring cylinder

____

Measuring tools

balancing scales

Mass as a tool

The mass of an object is the measure of how much matter it contains. Mass is measured in grams (g). To find the mass of an object, simple balancing scales are used to compare the unknown mass with a known mass. Electronic balances are used today.

Volume as a tool

The volume of an object is the measurement of the amount of space it occupies. It is measured in cubic lengths such as cubic metres (m^3) or cubic centimetres (cm^3).

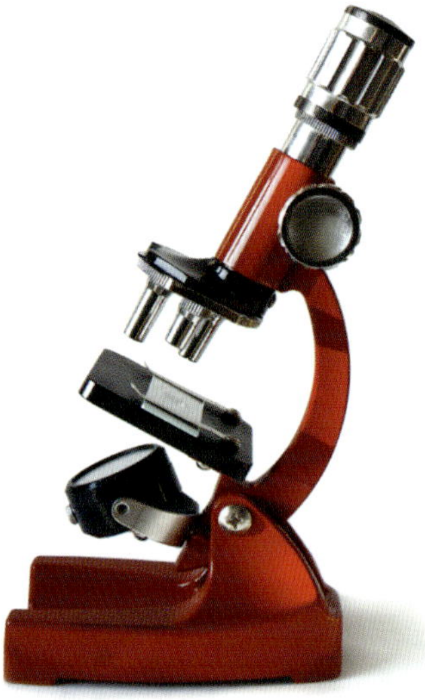

microsope

Magnification as a tool

Until the invention of the microscope, scientific study was limited to the examination and comparison of only visible physical features.

Computers as a tool

Computers are the brains that give electronic machines such as automatic pilots, robotic arms and television cameras their 'intelligence'. They also process data and do complicated calculations quickly. Scientists use computers to communicate information accurately and quickly, and the World Wide Web is a convenient source of information.

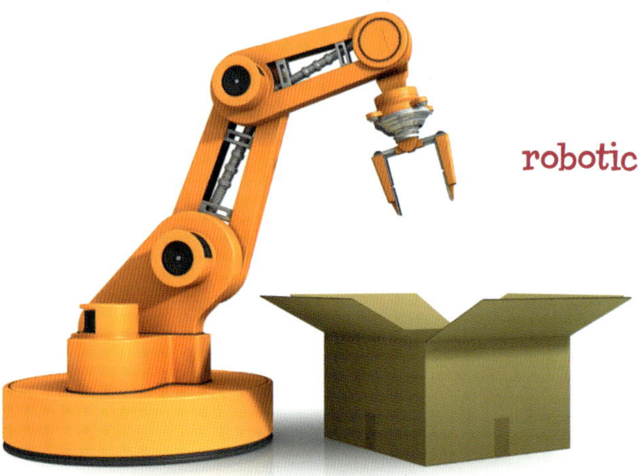

robotic arm

MEASURING AND RECORDING DATA

Science depends on an organised and careful collection of measurements. These measurements may be made in a controlled setting such as a laboratory or out in the field such as when measuring wild animal populations.
A collection of measurements is called data.

Units of measurement

Measurement is comparison. To compare objects, scientists use standard units of measurement for all variables. The units of measurement used should be suitable for the quantities involved in an experiment. For example, measuring the length of a frog in metres is too large a unit of measure. Some standard units of measurement are length: metres and liquid volume: litres.

To compare objects scientists use standard units of measurement

Recording measurements

Measurement error can occur in scientific experiments. Scientists check for errors by repeating an experiment and measurements several times and using averaging techniques.

In a laboratory, measurements are rarely written down haphazardly on a piece of paper. Measurements are usually recorded clearly in a table. A table must:

- have a clear title showing what the table is about
- have columns that are clearly labelled with headings
- use the correct units for measurements that are recorded.

Example
This table correctly displays the data about performance racing cars.

TABLE 1 Variation in time to reach 200km/hour with different car weights

Car weight (tonnes)	Time to reach a speed of 200km/hour (seconds)
0.5	20
1.0	40
1.5	60

Compare TABLE 1 above with the table shown. This table is a record of data about the growth of mice. List the four major mistakes made in this table.

Time	Weight
20	0.5
40	1.0
60	1.5

Try this

PROCESSING AND ANALYSING DATA

Data should be displayed in meaningful and useful ways so that trends, **patterns** and relationships can be identified. Data is the **evidence** used to justify **conclusions**.

Data handling skills

Scientists communicate in many ways. One way to present scientific information is in sketches or diagrams.

Example

Using diagrams of laboratory apparatus, maps, photographs and graphs; operating a piece of equipment and drawing an organism are all examples of presenting information without using words. Diagrams must always be drawn accurately and be clearly labelled. Sketches can be quick drawings without details.

Try this

White light bends when it passes through glass. White light is made up of many colours. These colours all travel at the same speed through air but when they pass through glass they slow down, each colour to a different speed.

Study the diagram of the glass prism below and answer the questions.

1 What do the lines represent?
2 What does the arrow represent?
3 According to the lines, which colour slows down the least?
4 Is this a diagram or a sketch?

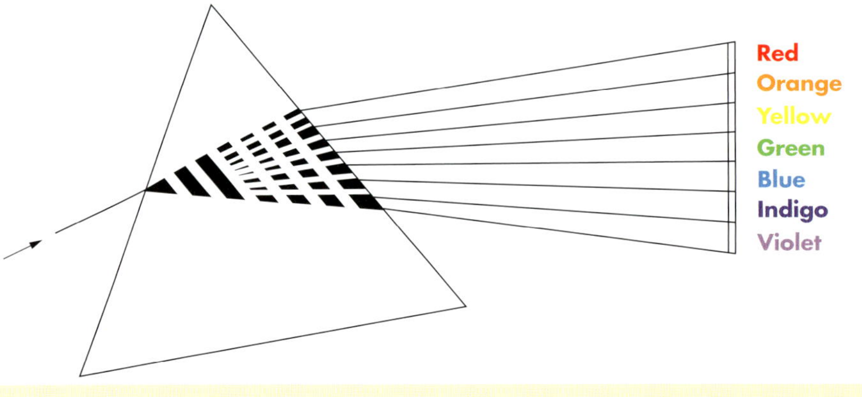

Graphing

A table is used to display data in an organised and easily understood way. This data is used to construct graphs. A graph is a visual way to compare data and communicate relationships between the data. Graphs are an essential part of understanding, **interpreting** and communicating the results of a scientific investigation.

Discrete and continuous data

The observations and measurements recorded in science experiments are recorded as discrete or continuous data. **Discrete data** is a certain value such as the number of students in a class (it must be a particular number). **Continuous data** is any value within a certain range such as the height of people (it can be variable and be measured in metres, centimetres or even millimetres).

Example

Discrete data is in categories such as gender, species of animal, brand of car and colour of lipstick. For example, how many bilbies live in this area?

Continuous data is measured using a standard unit with equal intervals. For example, the height of trees in metres (7.3 m), the amount of chocolate in grams (95.5 g) and the length of time to run in minutes (2.5 min).

Try this

The table below shows several variables. Determine whether each variable would be recorded as discrete data or continuous data.

Variable to be measured	
1	Length of time to run a marathon
2	Number of pizzas
3	'Mack' trucks on a highway
4	Temperature of the surf
5	Colours of nail polish

Appropriate graph format

There are many different ways to show the relationship between variables graphically. Selecting an appropriate graph format allows the information to be presented and interpreted in the best way.

To organise a graph:

- select an appropriate graph format
- arrange the information clearly
- design the graph so that it can be understood easily.

The information below summarises the main graph formats that are available.

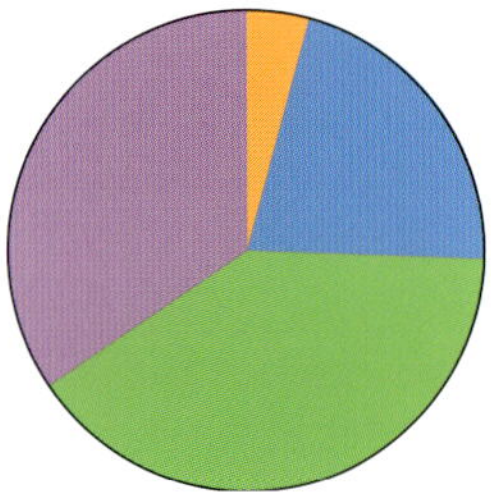

pie chart

Pie chart

A pie chart is a circle divided into sectors. The angles at the centre are in the same proportion as the numerical data. These graphs are used for displaying discrete data.

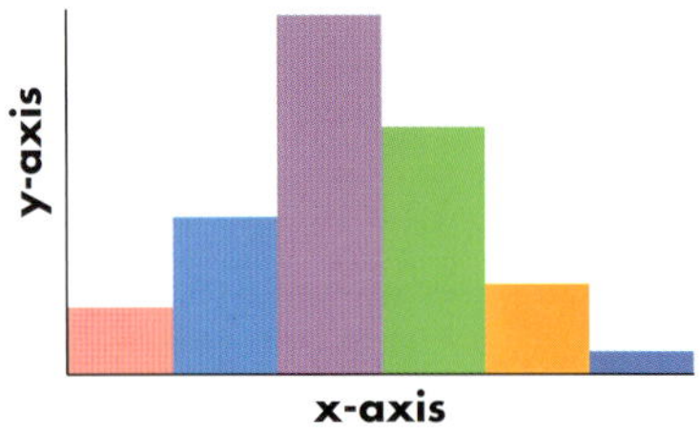

histogram

Histogram

A histogram has a horizontal axis that is marked in equal intervals. Columns are drawn to represent the numerical data. Adjacent columns have a common edge. These graphs show continuous data.

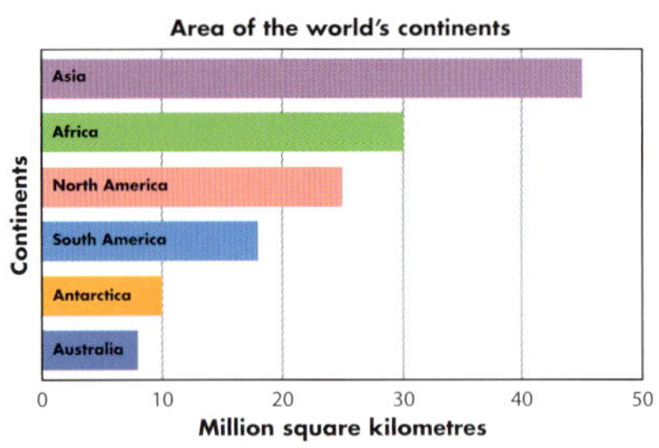

bar graph

Bar graph

A bar graph is used to compare several sets of results. They are used when one value is not numerical. These graphs show discrete data.

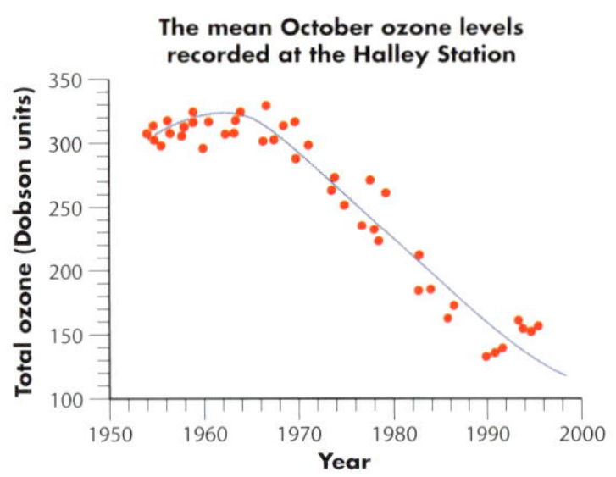

scatter graph

Scatter graph

A scatter graph is used for displaying the distribution of two variables. These variables may not have a dependent relationship with each other. These graphs show continuous data.

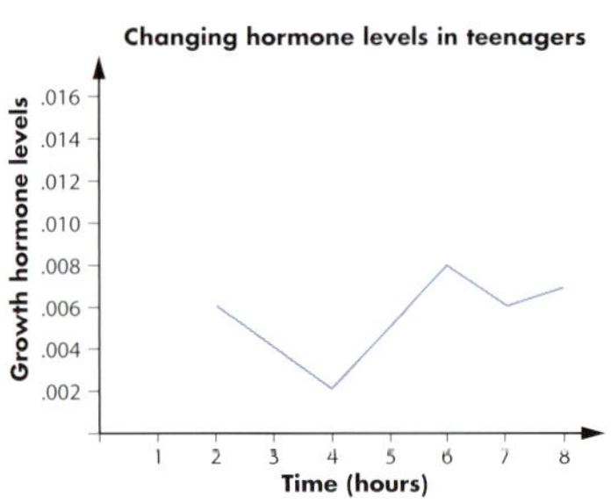

line graph

Line graph

A line graph is used for displaying the relationship between two variables. The data used are measurements over a period of time such as the temperature of a patient over a series of days.

These graphs show continuous data.

Column graph

A column graph has vertical columns of equal width that are drawn on the horizontal scale.

These columns are drawn to the appropriate height of the vertical scale. These graphs show discrete data.

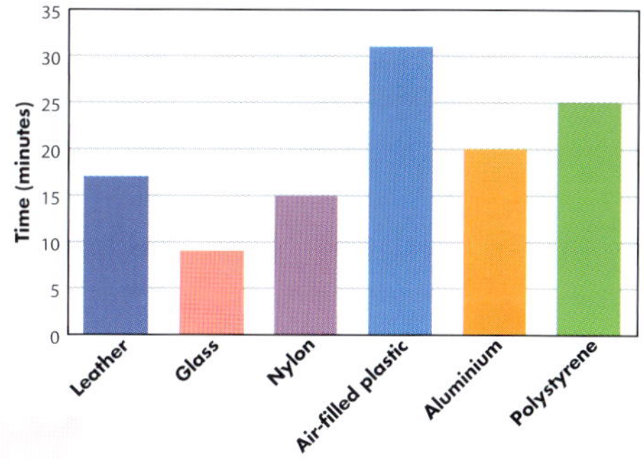

column graph

Example

The graph formats shown are most suitable for presenting the following data.

- *Pie chart – percentage of each bird species that make up the bird population of a national park*
- *Line graph – body weight of calves as they grow over twelve months*
- *Bar or column graph – average time that runners took to run four separate races*
- *Histogram – heights of students in a class*

Graphs can show a lot of information in a small space compared with verbal or written communication.

Fish caught in a trawler's net were sorted into different groups based on length. This information is recorded in the table below.

1 Which graph format would best represent this data?

2 If the fish had been grouped according to species instead of length, what graph format would you choose?

Table – Fish caught in trawler net

Length of fish (cm)	Number of fish caught
1–5	0
6–10	20
11–15	30
16–20	60
21–25	100
26–30	110
31–35	60
36–40	30
41–45	10
46–50	0
51–55	0

Try this

Rules for drawing a line graph

- The graph must have a title.
- The horizontal axis should display the independent variable (experimenter controls the cause).
- The vertical axis should display the dependent variable (experimenter measures the effect).
- The axes should be similar lengths and be clearly labelled with the variable that they represent.
- The axes should be labelled with the correct units of measurement.
- The scale on both axes should be in equal, ordered intervals and start from zero (the origin) where possible.
- If there is a large gap between zero and the first reading, on either axis, the axis can be broken immediately after the zero and before the first data. A mark of // should be shown across the axis where the break occurs.
- If points need to be plotted, plot each point accurately with an 'x' or a 'dot point'. Join the points with a line to demonstrate the trend. Unless it can be assumed to be correct, do not extend the line to the origin if the data does not start at zero. The origin is where the horizontal and vertical axes meet.

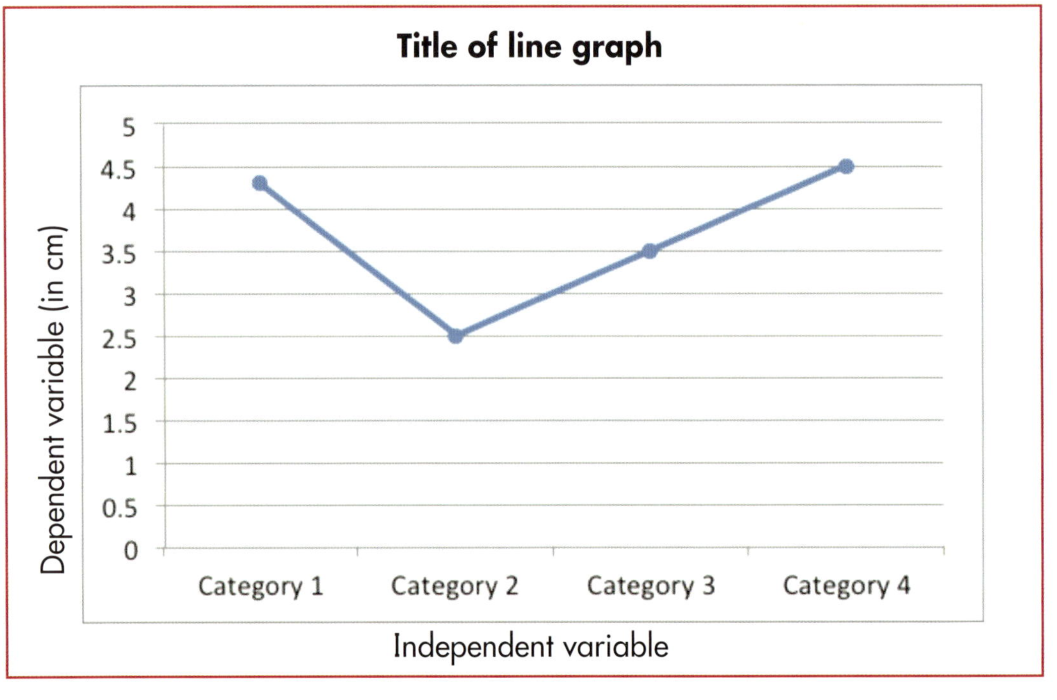

Example

Many rules have been broken when drawing Graph A and Graph B below.

Graph A describes the amount of food eaten by a wallaby between midnight and midday. Wallabies like to eat just before dawn.

Graph B describes the day's temperature for the 2.5-hour period following dawn.

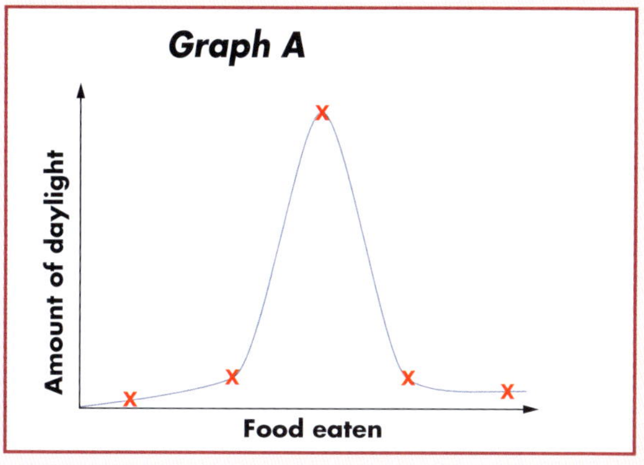

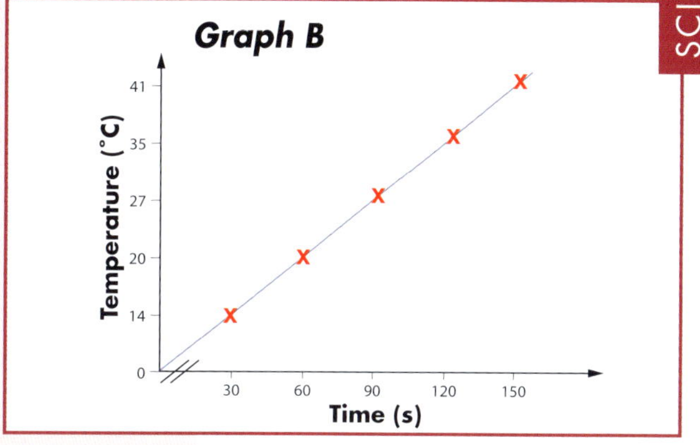

Mistakes for Graph A:

- *has no title*
- *horizontal axis should be time and the vertical axis should be the amount of food eaten*
- *graph is not labelled with units*
- *there is no scale on the horizontal or the vertical axis.*

Mistakes for Graph B:

- *has no title*
- *vertical axis is not an ordered scale*
- *there is no need to break the horizontal axis*

Try this

Refer to **Table – Fish caught in trawler net** on page 29.
Refer to the **Rules for drawing a line graph** listed on page 30.

1 What will the title of the graph be?
2 What will be shown on the horizontal axis?
3 What will the unit of measure be on the horizontal axis?
4 What will be shown on the vertical axis?
5 What will the unit of measure be on the vertical axis?
6 Draw a line graph correctly for the fish caught in a trawler net.
7 Why was a zero not required on the horizontal axis?
8 What percentage of the catch were more than 25 cm long?

EVALUATION

Scientists are constantly seeking evidence to support and prove their ideas and **predictions**. Science looks for connections in nature and patterns in data so they can understand and manage the natural world.

Data analysis and evaluation

Early humans had to search for patterns to survive. For example, knowing where food grew each year, when and where water was available, the times for fruiting and evidence of danger were all crucial to man's survival.

Scientists are no different when it comes to seeing cause and effect relationships and seeing the patterns of nature. The evidence must be of the highest quality so that the conclusion can be relied upon.

Example

Identifying patterns and working with patterns involves looking for relationships between things. The odd ones out in these lists are seagull (sea bird); bread (not a drink); and London (not in America)

- *galah, seagull, cockatoo, budgie*
- *wine, water, milk, bread, tea*
- *New York, Washington, San Francisco, London, Rio*

Try this

1 Which of the circles below does not fit the sequence?

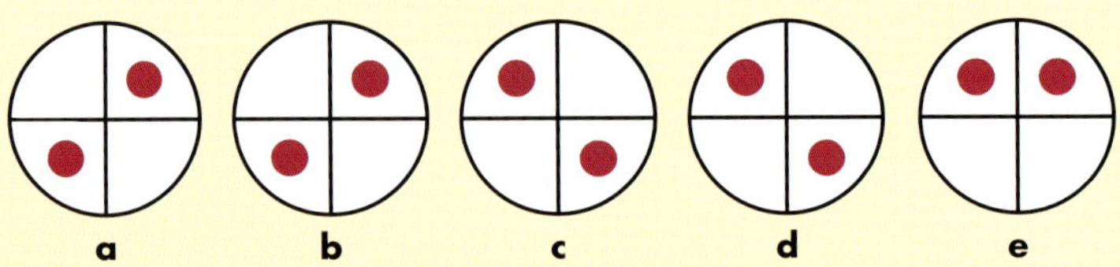

2 Examine the following series of letters:
XYYXZXYZXYYXZXY
What should the next three letters be?

Checklist for evaluating evidence

As an **investigation** is carried out, scientists note where improvements can be made.

In **evaluating** evidence, scientists search through their data looking for valid support for their predictions and explanations. Scientists:

- make relevant comments about the suitability of the method used
- comment on the accuracy and **reliability** of the results
- suggest changes to improve the reliability of the evidence
- find trends and patterns in the results and explain any results that do not fit the trend
- explain simply what was discovered – the conclusion
- decide if the evidence is good enough to support a firm conclusion.

Example

Scientists may use the following steps to evaluate data recorded in a graph.

1. ***Analyse*** *the data and respond to any questions raised by the data.*
2. ***Consider*** *the evidence and rank the data in order.*
3. ***Interpret*** *the collected evidence by carefully reading the data and developing a conclusion that can be supported.*
4. *Use* ***scientific knowledge*** *to explain a valid conclusion.*
5. ***Recommendations*** *can be made at this stage for changes in experimental design. Changes would be made to improve the method or the way that data was collected.*
6. ***Sources of error*** *are all the things that could affect the experimental outcome. These should be recognised. This includes poor use of controls, uncontrolled variables, and any error in reading meters and dials – commonly called human error.*
7. *Scientists make* ***suggestions*** *about other types of experiments that may relate to the one that they have done and that may be useful to other researchers.*

Try this

Cans of cold soft drink were each placed into similar containers made of each of the materials being investigated. The time taken for the temperature of the soft drink to rise by 5 degrees Celsius was recorded for each can. A column graph was drawn from the data.

Study the information presented in the graph (histogram) below and, based on the evidence, answer the questions.

Graph - Time taken for a cold can of soft drink in containers of insulating material to heat up by 5 degrees Celsius.

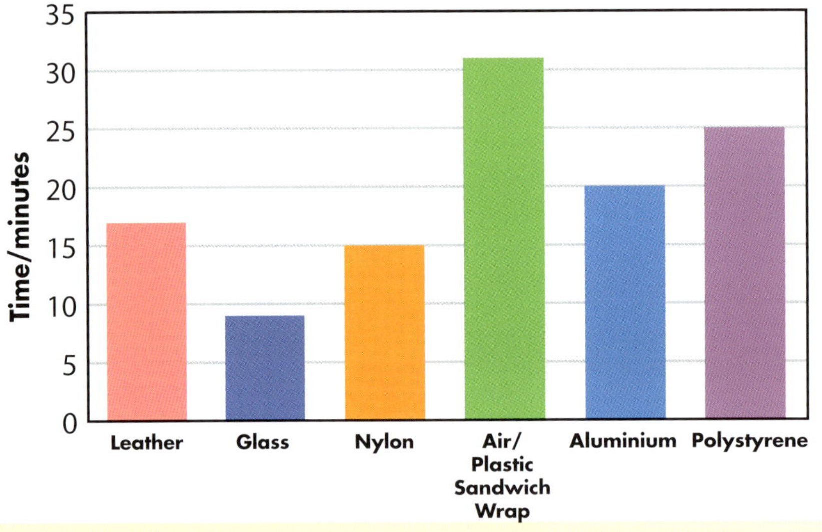

1 **Analyse** what has been discovered and answer the questions that follow.
   - **a** How many materials were tested?
   - **b** Which material allowed the soft drink to heat up the quickest?
   - **c** Which material kept the soft drink cold for the longest time?
   - **d** How long did it take for this can to heat up by 5 degrees Celsius?
   - **e** How much longer did the can in the aluminium container take to heat up than the can in the leather container?

2 **Consider** the evidence and rank the materials in order from the best insulator to the worst.

3 **Interpret** the evidence and extract a conclusion that you can support. Which is the best insulator?

4 Use **scientific knowledge** to explain the conclusion that you drew in question 3. Why do you think that polystyrene is also a good insulator?

5 **Recommend** what you would change in the experimental design of this experiment.

6 Write down some places in this investigation where **error** could be better minimised.

7 Write down one or two **suggestions** for other experiments that could be done to expand this line of **research**.

CONCLUSION

A conclusion is a summary of what you found out and sometimes what you did not find out.

A valid conclusion

Being able to draw a valid conclusion means that you have carefully considered questions such as:

- What were the results?
- What do they mean?
- Are they useful?
- What did you learn?

Results that have been carefully collected and recorded should show patterns and relationships that will make reaching a conclusion easier. We can compare the conclusion with the hypothesis and then answer the question: Does the data agree or disagree with your original guess (hypothesis)?

At this point, there are usually more questions to answer such as:

- Where does this information lead us?
- What do you need to investigate further?

Example

The following sentences about a house down the road have been marked with an ***O*** *for observation, a* ***H*** *for hypothesis or a* ***C*** *for conclusion.*

Observation: *something that you can see, hear, smell, touch or taste*

Hypothesis: *a possible explanation for something that has been observed*

Conclusion: *a summary of what you found out or did not find out*

The dog in the house down the road is barking. (O)
There could be someone walking by. (H)
The owners must be away. (C)

I heard the muffled sound of conversation. (O)
They may break into it tonight. (H)
Someone is assessing the house for a break-in. (C)

Try this

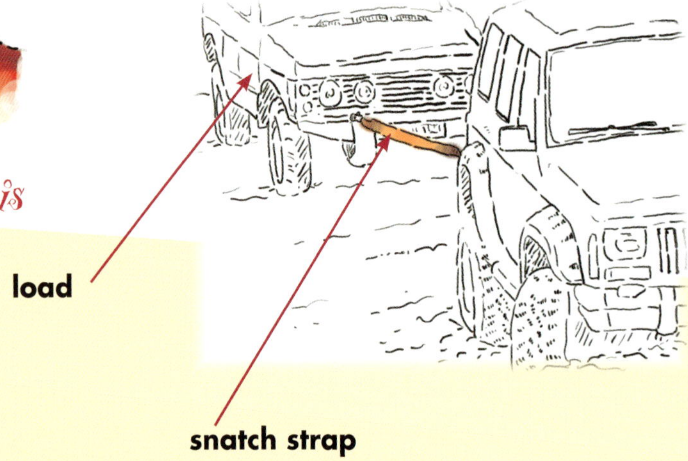

The graph shows the relationship between the extension of a snatch strap used to tow something behind a 4WD vehicle and the load that the snatch strap can tow behind a 4WD vehicle. A snatch strap is a type of tow rope.

The hypothesis being tested is:
Snatch strap extension is directly related to the load.

Graph of extension against load for a snatch strap

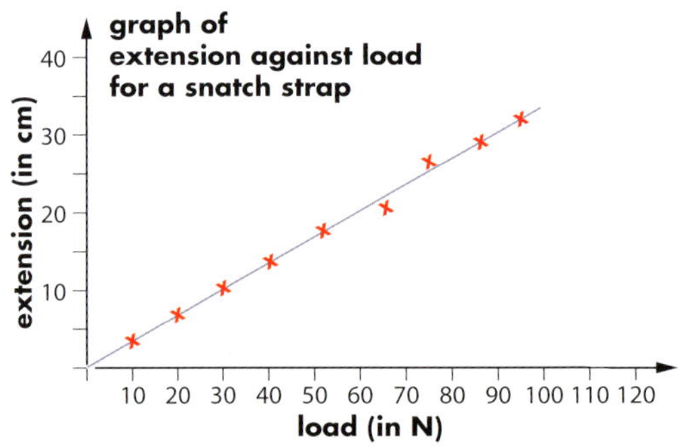

Observations:

- A line graph with a straight line through the origin indicates that the extension of the snatch strap is related to the load up to its elastic limit.
- The line indicates that as the load (the force required to get the car moving) increases the length of the snatch strap increases.

Study the graph and draw a valid conclusion from this data.

COMMUNICATING

Scientists tell other people about their work because it is important for other investigators to be able to test the same hypothesis independently. To do this they need to be able to follow the procedure exactly and have access to the original data. Reports are published in scientific journals so the format and style of the report should be the same as other reports in the journal.

Writing a report in scientific format

A scientific report usually is written to follow a standard format and is divided into several sections for easy reading and information that is clear.

Example

The following is an example of a format used for a simple scientific report.

Section	What information is included
Title	How do I describe the content of this report in the fewest number of words?
Introduction	Why am I doing it?
Review of literature	What do we know? What don't we know?
Aim / hypothesis	What do I hope to discover?
Method / equipment	How am I going to discover it? What equipment do I need?
Results	How do I display the data?
Discussion	What does it all mean?
Conclusion	What did I find out? What are the possible applications and recommendations? What next?

Try this

Use the rough laboratory notes below to write down the information required for each section of a scientific report, as shown above.

Laboratory notes:

- Find out about bicycle speeds over different terrain.
- Will the bicycle speed decrease going up the hill?
- Experiment: going up a hill with a sharp incline at the top, across the top and down the other side
- Speed to be recorded every two minutes for 10 minutes
- Stopwatch to measure the time and speed calculated
- At zero time, speed in km/h was 8, then followed 5, 0.5, 2.5, 7, 8

Checklist for report writing

There are other general rules for writing a scientific report. All scientific reports are written in the third person. This means that you must not write a report in terms of *I*, *you* or *we*. For instance, use the *researcher* instead of *I* and the *research team* instead of *us*.

Other rules for writing a scientific report:

- Avoid terms such as *in my opinion* – just state what was found out.
- Be precise in your use of language – use short active sentences.
- If you use scientific terms or acronyms that the reader may not know the meaning of, you should explain them either in the body of the report or in a glossary.
- Use bullet lists rather than lists in long sentences.

Example

Example A shows the incorrect way to list equipment; lists in a long sentence.
Example B shows the correct way to list equipment; in a bulleted list.

Example A

Equipment used includes a GPS, a 50m tape, quadrant markers, a plant identification guide and pH testing kits.

Example B

Equipment:

- *GPS*
- *50 m tape*
- *quadrant markers*
- *plant identification guide*
- *pH testing kits*

Try this

Rewrite the scientific report shown below according to the rules above.

Scientific Report

My friend and I want to find out which plants are still growing where the pH of the soil has been increased by alkaline runoff from a building site.
We gathered together things like a GPS, a pH meter and a plant identification book. We took the long way around to the site, as it was a lovely walk.
When we got there, I decided to record the plants that we found in each quadrant and my friend recorded the pH values. We also noted the exact location of each quadrant using the GPS and the tape measure. In our opinion, the high pH levels stopped the growth of only some plants.

BIOLOGICAL SCIENCES

Biological sciences develop knowledge and understanding about living things.
For example: cells, plants, animals, bacteria and fungi

We share the planet with many other living organisms

BIOLOGY – THE STUDY OF LIFE

Looking at life

Humans may dominate the natural world, but we share the planet with many other living organisms. We are part of a huge web of life. By understanding the natural world, scientists help us to live without damaging nature.

The condition of being alive

The study of life is termed **biology**. The fundamental questions for biologists are:

- What makes something alive?
- How does it survive in a constantly changing world?

A **living organism** is anything that has these characteristics.

- respiration
- excretion
- **reproduction**
- nutrition
- growing and developing
- sensitivity to things around us.

Organisms range in size, from microscopic bacteria to giant whales. An organism's **life cycle** is a pattern of change during its lifetime – it grows, develops, reproduces and dies. The life cycle of an insect may be ten days. But the life cycle of an elephant may be seventy years. Organisms stay alive by juggling chemicals. **Death** occurs when this chemical juggling act stops and the organism's **cells** break down. Death is the end of an organism but is important for **evolution** to proceed from generation to generation.

Organisms stay alive by juggling chemicals

A fresh apple on a tree is alive. What do we do to apples to stop them being alive?

Try this

Example

The basic processes that make living things alive are:

- *getting and using food (nutrition)*
- *removing waste (excretion)*
- *reproduction*
- *releasing energy (respiration)*
- *growth*

A living thing is alive until its chemical processes stop and then it is no longer alive – it is dead

An anatomist studies the structure of living things, how they fit together and how they are linked through evolution. Anatomists use special terms to guide them to the location of animal features.

Example

Ventral is underneath the body
Dorsal is the back of the body
Anterior is the front of the body
Posterior is behind the body
Lateral is the side of the body

Try this

What features are found on the ventral, dorsal, anterior, posterior and lateral locations of this fish?

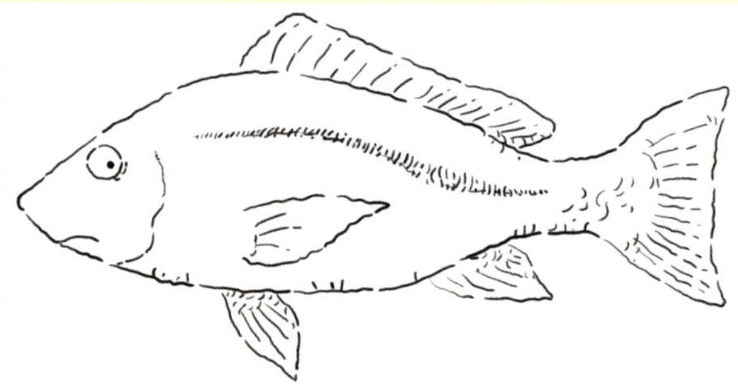

Cells: the basic unit of life

Cells are tiny self-contained units, which are the basic building blocks of all living things. Some organisms are just one individual cell, like an amoeba. Other organisms, like humans, consist of thousands of billions of cells.

All living things grow and change during their lives. The **nucleus** of a cell is the cell's control centre and contains the entire organism's genetic information. The cell takes in energy and uses it to develop and reproduce. Cells reproduce by dividing into two. This cell division increases the number of cells in the organism. However, to produce a new plant or animal a male and a female sex cell must join together. This is called **fertilisation**.

Plant cells are slightly different from animal cells in that they contain **chloroplasts**. These are like tiny solar panels full of green chlorophyll that allow the plant to capture the energy from the sun and make its own food.

Cells have different structure and functions but when combined, produce the endless variety of nature. These cells can be arranged in groups (tissues) and carry out different jobs for the organism.

Example

Most cells are different in structure and function. Some cells are similar so that they can work together to perform a particular function in the body.

Try this

Match the cell group with each of the following: heart, digestive system, muscle.

1 A tissue is a group of similar cells that work together such as the skin.
2 An organ is a structure made of more than one type of tissue and carries out a particular job in the human body such as the lungs.
3 A system is a group of organs working together such as the nervous system.

The chemistry of life

Chemicals are not just found in laboratories. All living things are made up of simple and complex chemicals that react with one another. These chemical activities are collectively called **metabolism**. The energy required for these activities is obtained by the breakdown of food substances.

Life on Earth is based on the element carbon

Life on Earth is based on the element carbon. Carbon atoms combine with atoms of other elements to form organic compounds. There are four main organic compounds in living things that are based on carbon.

1 **Carbohydrates** are produced by plants. They are made up of carbon, hydrogen and oxygen and are essential sources of energy for all living things.
2 **Lipids, fats and oils** store energy and provide insulation for an organism. Waxes and oils provide waterproofing and scents for plants.
3 **Proteins** perform many functions in living things such as controlling chemical reactions. They also build structures such as hair, fingernails and muscle.
4 **Nucleic acids** (DNA) carry the organism's genetic information, which is stored in the nucleus of cells.

Classification of life

As scientists explore the world, they love to sort living things into groups according to similarities and differences. Classification, or grouping, requires observation and attention to detail. Classifying involves comparing, describing and naming the living thing.

Example

To classify your clothing you look for differences and similarities and may use groups such as dirty clothes on the floor and clean clothes in the ironing basket, some shoes under the bed and others in the cupboard, and all socks jumbled together or matched into pairs based on colour.

Try this

Each organism on Earth has its own special characteristics.

Ben has eyes with short lashes, blonde hair and dimples. He can raise one eyebrow at a time but he cannot roll his tongue into a lengthwise tube. Ben's mum has blonde hair, long lashes, but no dimples. Ben's dad has brown hair, short lashes and dimples. Both parents can roll their tongue but only Ben's dad can raise one eyebrow.

Using the columns in the table below, tick the traits that Ben inherited from his father and those that he inherited from his mother. What is your own special characteristic?

Trait	Ben's characteristics	Ben's mother	Ben's father
Hair	Blonde		
Dimples	Yes		
Eye lashes	Short		
Ability to roll your tongue into a lengthwise tube	No		
Ability to raise one eyebrow only	Yes		

Special characteristic ______________________________

Classification system

The classification system for living things is based on five kingdoms: monerans (bacteria), protists (protozoa, amoeba), fungi (mushrooms, mould), plants and animals. However, scientists classify most living things into one of the two greatest kingdoms: the plant kingdom or the animal kingdom.

Example

When you classify things, you must look beyond what you can actually see.

For example: We can see that dolphins and sharks are streamlined so that they can move through water to catch food. However, scientists classify sharks as 'fish' and dolphins as 'mammals'.

The following features place sharks and dolphins into different groups. Sharks breathe with gills and their flippers have stiff rods made of cartilage. Dolphins breathe with lungs and their flippers have bones arranged in rows like finger bones.

Try this

There are many ways to sort living things. Sort the animals and plants in the drawing below into the following categories.

Category	Plants and animals
Plants	
Animals that live in water	
Animals that do not live in water	
Animals with bones	
Animals without bones	
Animals that are eaten by other animals	

A

B

C

D

E

F

G

H

I

Putting a name to it

When a life form is classified, biologists describe it and give it a scientific name. This name identifies it and shows which group it belongs to in the living world. Names are often based on the unique characteristics of the life form or the place where the life form grows.

When a life form is classified, it is given a two-part scientific name, called a **binomial name**. This name consists firstly of a genus name and secondly a species name.

Example

The scientific or binomial name for the Eastern Grey Kangaroo is Macropus giganteus. This name means 'big feet'. The genus name is macropus and the species name is giganteus. The common name is the Eastern Grey Kangaroo.

Try this

When the very first platypus reached England in 1799, zoologists and taxomists of the time were baffled. They thought the creature was a fraud and a hoax – someone was having a huge joke.

The platypus was furred, warm-blooded, suckled its young like a mammal but had a bill and laid eggs like a bird. This unique combination of characteristics confused the naturalist's views on classifying animals.

The scientists of Europe argued for years about which group to classify this odd animal. It was classified, along with the echidna, in the group monotremes, meaning 'one hole' for egg laying and removal of wastes.

In 1836, Charles Darwin was actually able to study the elusive platypus near Bathurst in New South Wales. More recently, scientists have discovered that the platypus has electro sensors on its bill that help it to find food.

1 What is the name of the animal group into which scientists finally placed the platypus?
2 What is the only other Australian animal that has been classified as belonging to this same group?
3 What recently discovered, invisible characteristic does the platypus have?
4 If the platypus and the echidna have been classified into the same group, then what new characteristic would scientists expect to find in the echidna?

PLANT KINGDOM

What do plants do?

- produce oxygen
- absorb carbon dioxide
- filter out dust
- act as windbreaks
- moderate temperature
- reduce noise
- create natural beauty
- increase underground water resources
- provide food and shelter for wildlife
- provide food, oils, wood and paper for humans
- provide fibre for clothing and other materials
- cover and protect soil
- provide shade

Plant groups

Algae are the simplest form of plants. They live wherever there is water, sunlight and a supply of nutrients. Like all plants, **algae** use the sun's energy to make food and are food for other life forms.

Non-flowering plants do not have flowers and do not produce seeds. They are some of the oldest plants on Earth. Most non-flowering plants spread by producing small packs of cells called spores. Algae, seaweed, mosses, liverworts and ferns are all non-flowering plants. They live either in water or in places where there is plenty of moisture.

Seed plants reproduce by making seeds. **Gymnosperms** or conifers are primitive seed plants, depending on the wind for fertilisation. They produce seeds without a protective coating 'naked seeds'.

Flowering plants, or **angiosperms**, are the most successful plants on Earth as they have evolved side by side with insects. This evolution ensures a precise fertilisation of the flowers by the insects. Seeds are produced inside a protective structure such as a fruit, pod or nut.

Example

The coconut plant produces a seed in a shell. The plant is used by Asian communities to supply many of their needs such as food, housing, furniture.

The tallest tree in Australia is the Mountain Ash *(Eucalyptus regnans)* which grows to a height of 90 metres.

Try this

1. **Which of the following are seed plants:** pine trees, palm trees, kelp, fruit trees, lettuce, and moss?
2. **What do we use pine trees for?**

Plant structure

Plants need different structures from animals because they make their own food from the sun; and water, air and nutrients from the soil – they photosynthesise.

Organs of a plant

- **Leaf** A plant organ that intercepts light and exchanges gases.
- **Stem** Gives the plant structure and supports the buds, leaves and flowers.
- **Root** Takes in water and minerals from the soil and holds the plant in the soil.
- **Bud** An undeveloped shoot that is protected by scales and grows into new flowers or leaves.
- **Flower** A structure that contains the male and female organs for reproduction in flowering plants.
- **Seed** A reproductive structure containing a plant embryo and a food store.
- **Fruit** A ripened case that contains and protects the seeds of a plant.

Transport tissues

Inside plants, substances are always moving around from place to place.

- **Xylem** is a plant tissue, where cells are joined together to form long pipelines inside the plant. These tubes transport water and minerals from the soil to all parts of the plant.
- **Phloem** is a tissue that carries the food from the leaves to the rest of the plant.
- The food is manufactured in the leaves by photosynthesis.

Example

When we eat spinach, lettuce, cabbage we are eating leaves. Broccoli and cauliflower are flowers. Asparagus, potatoes and celery are stems. Carrots, turnips and beetroot are roots. Brussels sprouts are buds. Coconuts, peanuts, popcorn, peas and rice are seeds. Apples, corn and pineapples are fruits.

Try this

Label the plant diagram with the following features: leaf, flower, stem, root, bud.

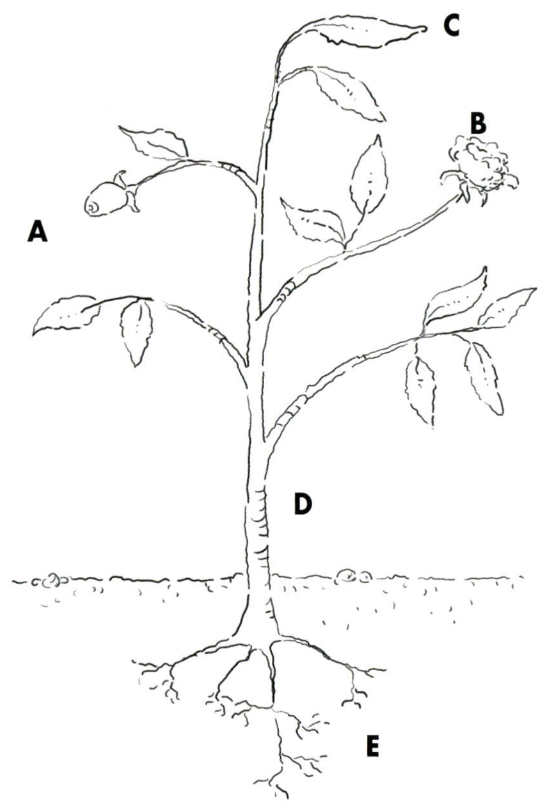

Plant processes

A physiologist studies how the processes in living things work. Plants work by two processes: photosynthesis and transpiration.

Photosynthesis

Photosynthesis is a process where plants use light energy to make food from simple chemicals. This process provides food for almost every living thing. The foods produced are simple sugars like glucose and fructose.

Plants make their own food using energy from the sun

Some of this food is used straight away by the plant. Some of the food is sent off for storage in places like roots (carrots) and stems (potato). Some of the food is used to grow more of the plant such as leaves, stems, roots and flowers.

Chlorophyll is the main pigment in plants and is used for photosynthesis. Chlorophyll collects the sun's energy and gives plants their green colour.

Transpiration

Plants lose water vapour by evaporation through the **stomata** of the leaves. This water is replaced by water from the roots and travels through the xylem. This process is called transpiration. The rate of transpiration, or how fast water is lost, depends on the atmosphere. Temperature, humidity, water content of the air and how fast the air is moving (wind) all affect transpiration.

A large rainforest tree can pump out as much as 900 litres of water through its leaves on a hot day. Plants that live in dry, windy places have other features such as small leaves, few stomata or a covering of hairs to protect the leaf surface and reduce water loss.

Example

Transpiration is a process where water is absorbed through the roots and travels through the xylem.
The water vapour is eventually lost through the leaves.
Plants have different features to cope with the conditions in which they live.

An experiment on transpiration was set up as shown and left for five days.

A: both surfaces coated with Vaseline

B: the lower leaf surface coated with Vaseline

C: the upper leaf surface coated with Vaseline

Which tube – A, B or C – will have the least water after five days?

A few years ago, the Space Shuttle took seeds into space to see how zero gravity would affect germination and growth.

Use the explanation of geotropism to predict how the seeds would have behaved at germination and during growth, while on the Space Shuttle.

Plant growth

Most plants grow slowly and can become very large. Some parts of plants grow to a certain size like flowers and leaves. But other parts, like stems and roots, may keep growing for all of the plant's life.

Life cycle of a plant

1 **Germination** of a seed.
2 The stem begins to grow upwards and away from gravity.
3 A small root breaks through the seed coat and grows towards gravity.
4 The first leaves emerge above the ground and begin to collect energy.
5 The plant grows bigger and bigger.
6 A flower is produced and pollination occurs.
7 Seeds develop inside the fruits.
8 The fruits fall from the plant to the ground.

Example

When a plant is beginning to peek out from the seed, it is said to be 'sprouting'. Beans, peas and other plants can be eaten when they are sprouting.
On Earth, when the seed sprouts, roots always grow towards gravity (positively geotropic) and leaves always grow away from gravity (negatively geotropic).

Plant reproduction

Plants produce flowers, which, no matter what their shape, colour or size, have the same structures. The flower's main function is to achieve pollination so that it is able to produce seeds for reproduction.

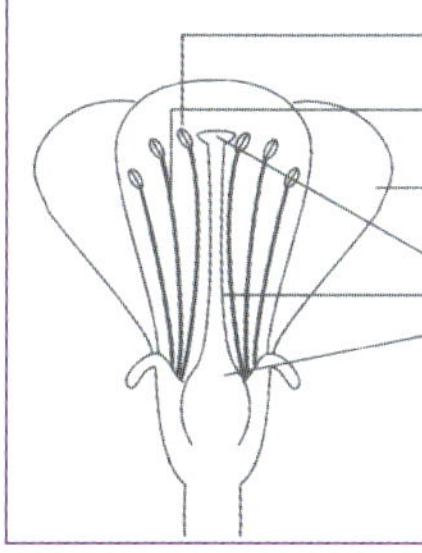

Parts of a flower

Flowers contain the organs of sexual reproduction in plants. There are many parts, each part has a job to do.

- The large, brightly coloured **petals**, combined with the perfume of the flower are an effective attractant for pollinators.
- The **stamen** is the male, pollen producing part of the flower. It is made up of an anther (a tiny bag-like structure full of pollen) and a filament (a small stalk on which rests the anther).
- The **pistil** is the female, seed bearing part of the flower. It consists of a sticky stigma and a sac called an ovary, which houses the seeds.

Pollination

Pollination occurs when a pollen grain is transferred by insects, birds or the wind from the stamen (male part) of one flower to the stigma (female part) of another. Wind pollinated plants like grasses and conifers have no need for colour or perfume. Plants pollinated by insects are usually large, brightly coloured and sweet smelling. Insects visit flowers to collect the nectar and by default deliver the pollen. Once pollination has occurred, the flower dies back as the seeds develop.

Plants pollinated by insects are usually large, brightly coloured and sweet smelling.

Example

The coloured petals of flowers are a clever way that plants attract birds and insects. The male 'stamen' is the pollen producing part of the flower. The female 'pistil' is the seed bearing part of the flower. Once pollen has been transferred, the petals die back and a seed develops.

Try this

Bees spend much of their time rummaging around inside a flower, busily collecting nectar. However, bees always seem to be heavily dusted with yellow pollen from the flower's stamens. **How do bees help with pollination and seed production?**

ANIMAL KINGDOM

The blue whale is the largest animal in the world.

An animal is any living organism other than a plant. Animals are sorted into two two main groups, invertebrates and vertebrates.

Animal groups

Invertebrates

An invertebrate is an animal that does not have a backbone. Invertebrates make up 90% of all animal species. The following groups are some of the invertebrates.

- **Worms** have long soft bodies and no legs. Examples are earthworms, tapeworms and leeches.
- **Molluscs** are invertebrates that have soft, moist bodies often protected by hard shells. Examples are oysters, snails, squid and octopus.
- **Echinoderms** are invertebrates with spiny skins and a five-part body plan. Examples are starfish, sea urchins and sea squirts.

- **Arthropods** are invertebrates with a jointed body case, which is tough and waterproof. Arthropods are the largest and most successful group in the animal kingdom. Examples are crabs, lobsters, spiders, centipedes and insects.

- **Insects** are a subgroup of the arthropods, and outnumber all the other living creatures on Earth combined. They have six legs and a body divided into three parts. Examples are grasshoppers, dragonflies, beetles, butterflies and termites.

Vertebrates

Vertebrates are animals that do have a backbone. Most vertebrates also have highly developed, sense organs and nervous systems so that they can react to their surroundings.

- **Fish** are the most successful group of vertebrates. They live in the water and are equipped with slippery scales, a streamlined body and a swim bladder to keep them afloat. Examples are bony fish like flathead and mackerel; cartilaginous fish like sharks, eels and lungfish.

- **Amphibians** were the first vertebrates to develop legs instead of fins so that they could live on land as well as in the water. Examples are frogs, toads and salamanders.

- **Reptiles** were the first animals to become fully successful on land. They have a scaly skin and sealed, soft-shelled eggs and are cold blooded (ectothermic). Examples are lizards, snakes, turtles and crocodiles.
- **Birds** are animals with feathers. They are the most successful flying animal, have hard-shelled eggs and are warm blooded (endothermic). *Examples are owls, waders, emus, parrots and eagles.*
- **Mammals** have hair, feed their young milk and are warm blooded. Examples are kangaroos, platypuses, whales, rodents and humans.

The tallest land mammal is the giraffe, standing at 6 metres high.

Example

Invertebrates make up 90% of all animal species. Insects are one group of invertebrates. One group of vertebrates is the mammals. Australian placental mammals are a group of animals that include bush rats, dolphins and flying foxes.

Try this

Here is a pie graph of groups of living organisms that are presently known.

1 Which two groups of organisms dominate the Earth?

2 What percentage of all known species (1 413 000) do the fungi make up?

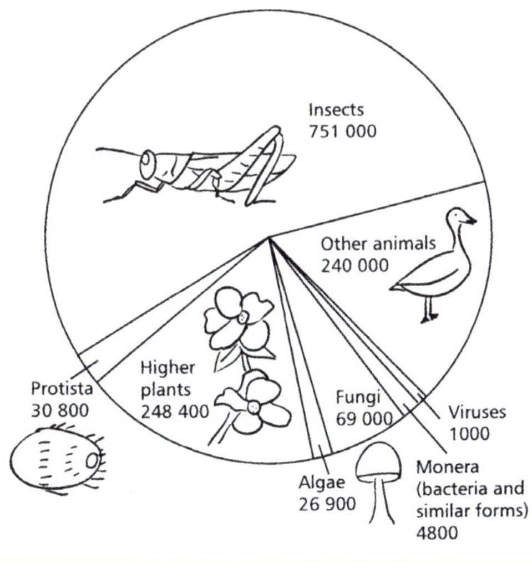

BIOLOGICAL SCIENCES

Animals only survive if all their systems are working together.

Animal systems

Animal systems are an ordered collection of processes, with inputs and outputs. Each system has an identity separate from the rest of the animal. Animals only survive if all their systems are working together.

- The **skin** is the largest organ of the body in most vertebrates. The skin is a tough, waterproof barrier that protects the body against harmful bacteria, the sun's rays and injury. Outgrowths of the skin include hair, fingernails and scales.
- The **nervous system** enables an animal to react to its surrounding environment. Nerves send messages from one part of the body through the brain to another.
- The **digestive system** breaks down food from large chunks into simple substances that can be used by the body.
- The **circulatory system** carries blood around the body. Blood carries nutrients, oxygen, hormones and wastes.
- The **respiratory system** is a gas exchange system. Animal cells need to take in oxygen and exhale out carbon dioxide.
- The **skeletal system** is a framework, that supports an animal's body and to which muscles are attached.
- The **muscular system** allows animals to move around.
- The **reproductive system** gives all living things the capacity to increase their numbers by producing offspring.
- The **excretory system** involves sweat, carbon dioxide and urine. Faeces are not excreted, as it never gets inside the body – it just goes through a long tube (digestive tract) from the mouth to the anus.

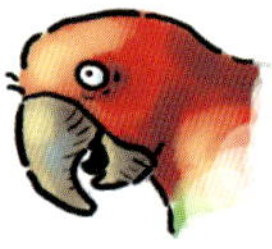

Try this

If you accidently put your hand on a hot stove, which systems would need to co-ordinate together to remove your hand from the heat?

Example

The body systems often work together or in tandem. The digestive, circulatory, and excretory systems are responsible for transporting materials around animal bodies. The muscular and skeletal systems work together and allow an animal to move.

Animal processes

Homeostasis

Homeostasis is the balance of conditions in a cell or a living thing. The internal environment of every living organism must be kept within certain limits. Control systems in a living thing correct unwanted changes. The respiratory system balances oxygen and carbon dioxide, and water and salt content are balanced by the kidneys.

Thermoregulation

Thermoregulation is the control and adjustment of body temperature. The body temperature of an **ectotherm** (cold blooded) can change with its surroundings. **Endotherms** (warm blooded) such as mammals and birds maintain a constant body temperature by generating heat through their metabolism. They modify environmental change through **sweating**, **shivering**, **vasodilation** and **insulation**.

Example

Reptiles, fish and amphibians are ectothermic, they move into or out of the sun to regulate their body temperature. Whales are endothermic and have huge amounts of blubber to insulate them from the cold of the oceans.

Try this

The human body relies on the heat produced by burning food to keep its internal organs at an optimum certain temperature. What is the one factor common to all of the following heat regulation processes?

- We get goose bumps on our skin when we get cold
- Wearing several layers of clothing in cold climates
- Using a sleeping bag to keep warm
- Wearing a lined, waterproof suit in the snow
- Igloos are made of snow, not ice

Animal growth

A life cycle is a predictable pattern of changes during the life of an organism. At the beginning of its life, a living thing like a plant grows and develops. When it reaches a particular age or size, it begins to reproduce and then it starts to die.

Metamorphosis

Metamorphosis is a type of life cycle where a total change in body shape occurs as an animal matures into an adult. Many animals start life as free-living larva and then change into adults with entirely different body shapes.

A tadpole is the larva of a frog. The tadpole lives in water, eats plants, breathes through gills and has a long tail instead of legs. As it grows its gills shrink, become covered with flaps of skin and then lungs develop. The tadpole slowly becomes a carnivore. Tiny legs appear as its tail shrinks. In its final preparation for life on land, its lungs and legs grow quickly and its tail disappears.

Example

A caterpillar is the wingless larva of a moth or butterfly. It hatches from an egg. A caterpillar has a large head and strong jaws because it feeds on tough plant material. It uses camouflage to blend into its surroundings and bright warning colours or irritating hairs for protection. The resting stage of these organisms is inside a tough case called a pupa. In the pupa stage, the larva forms a new, hard, shiny skin called a chrysalis. Inside, the caterpillar's cells break down and new cells form. An adult butterfly or moth then emerges with a totally changed body shape.

What special features (adaptations) do caterpillars have that help them to survive during this stage of the butterfly's life cycle?

Try this

Animal feeding

Animals need food substances to get the energy needed to survive. **Feeding** is the process of taking in food. Animals have different diets and ways of feeding to meet their lifestyles and nutritional needs. Once the food is taken in, it is slowly broken down by the digestive process.

Single-celled animals, such as amoeba, flow around the food and engulf it. Multi-celled animals have special body parts (jaws and teeth) that help them to take in food.

A **diet** is the type of food an animal eats. Some animals have a diverse diet whilst others eat a narrow range of food. For example, a koala eats only eucalypt leaves. The amount of food an animal eats depends on its size and its metabolic rate.

Type of animals and what they eat

- **Herbivores** are animals that eat only plant food. They have special teeth for grinding tough plant material. Many have a special digestive system to break down plants. Herbivores have to eat lots of food to get enough nutrients.
- **Carnivores** eat mostly meat. Most carnivores are predators and survive by hunting other animals. They have features such strong jaws or beaks and canine teeth. They eat small amounts and survive for a long time between meals.
- **Omnivores** eat plants and animals by tearing and chewing with tough teeth.
- **Detritus feeders** eat the remains of dead animals and plants. Some use claws to tear the food. They are often found on the sea floor or the forest floor. They are critical in the nutrient recycling process.
- **Filter feeders** collect microscopic plants and animals suspended in the water around them by sieving it out.

Herbivores are animals that eat only plant food

Carnivores eat mostly meat.

Example

The table provides examples of animals and their diet.

	Herbivore	Carnivore	Omnivore	Detritus feeder	Filter feeder
Animal	cow, goat, horse, wallaby	sharks, lions, birds of prey, snakes	humans, chickens, bears	crabs, prawns	barnacles, baleen whales, oysters
Main diet	plants	animals	plants and animals	remains of dead animals and plants	suspended nutrients from water

Complete the table below with one special feature that assists the feeder to ingest food.

Herbivore	Carnivore	Omnivore	Detritus feeder	Filter feeder

Animal movement

Animals have features that are adapted for survival in the habitats in which they live. Moving within the habitat is required for finding food, partners, shelter and an escape route from predators. Some animals like vertebrates move around a lot, using muscles for jet propulsion (squid), to swim (penguin), to slither (snake), to walk, to jump (fleas), to fly and to hover. Simple animals move by beating cilia or by amoeboid action.

The senses are the animal's radar system

Animal senses

The senses are the animal's radar system. The senses collect information about the animal's surroundings so that it can respond quickly and adjust its behaviour. This information is collected by the sense organs and transmitted to the brain via nerves for interpretation.

The five senses are:

- **Vision** detects light. The eye is the organ that allows animals to see their surroundings. For some animals it is the most important sense.
- **Hearing** detects sound. The ear is the organ that collects sound waves so the animal can detect food and danger, and can communicate. The inner ear detects gravity and therefore balance.
- **Touch** detects contact via nerve endings in the skin.
- **Taste** detects dissolved chemicals. Taste permits animals to test whether a food is good or bad for it to eat.
- **Smell** detects airborne chemicals. The molecules must waft through the air and up a nose before they can be detected.

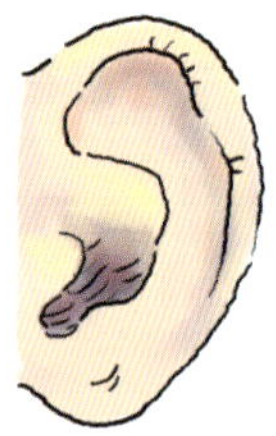

Example

Animals, including humans use their senses to make sure that food is safe to eat. Touch detects prickly and slimy materials, smell senses revolting odours, sight tells us if food looks too awful to eat and taste detects bitter or hot foods.

Try this

Animals use their senses for finding food, so their senses are adapted to the time of day that they hunt. Complete the following table by adding the senses used to find food.

Animal	dingo	bat	owl	eagle
Sense				

Animal communication

Animals use communication to exchange information. They keep in touch, warn rivals to go away and warn others of approaching danger. Complex forms of communication are used by animals that live in communities such as bees, ants and termites. Animals use many ways to communicate.

Example

The table provides examples of communication between animals.

Form of communication	Example
Touch	Used by those that live under ground, between parents and their offspring and during courtship
Chemical	The release of scents into the air or water to attract mates, to mark territories and to recognise each other
Sound / vocal cords	Used by animals such as grasshoppers, birds, and mammals. Humans can formulate words and language
Vision	Communication that revolves around movement (facial expressions and body language), colours (male birds, insects) and shapes

Try this

Honeybees communicate by dancing. Bees dance to tell other worker bees not only how far to fly but in which direction to find nectar supplies. A dance circle 2 centimetres in diameter means food is 10 metres away, an oval dance means 100 metres and a figure of eight means more than 100 metres. The angle of the waist in the figure of eight indicates the position of the food relative to the sun (vertical means directly towards the sun).

Study the bee dances below.

1 Is the food closest to bee 1 or bee 2?

2 How far is the food and in which direction is it from bee 3?

Animal behaviour

An animal's behaviour helps it to survive and to reproduce.

An animal's behaviour is a response to the surrounding world. It is not only what it does but also how it does it. An animal's behaviour helps it to survive and to reproduce. Some forms of behaviour are inherited (instinctive) such as building a nest or a web. Some of the animal's behaviours are learned through life experience. These behaviours are flexible and allow animals to adapt to their environment.

Example

The examples in the table demonstrate forms of animal behaviour.

Behaviour	Example
Circadian rhythm is a 24-hour cycle involving day and night behaviours.	Owls and possums sleep during the day and hunt at night.
Hibernation occurs when the animal's body temperature drops and the metabolic rate slows in order to survive a winter.	Polar bears and some reptiles hibernate.
Migration is animal movement in response to the seasons. A changing food supply or a more favourable environment to raise offspring triggers long journeys.	Many birds, mammals, fish and insects embark on long trips.
Territory establishment is usually in response to competition for food, a mate or somewhere to raise young.	Scrub turkeys defend an area, with aggressive behaviour and fighting.
Courtship is a behaviour that occurs before breeding and forms a bond between a male and a female.	Rainforest birds use signalling and complex body movements.
Parental care ranges from being absent all together or involving long periods of intensive care. Some animals just produce many offspring in the hope that some will survive.	Lizards lay eggs and never return to the site whereas mammals care for their offspring for a long time.
Social behaviour is how animals share the care of the young, the collection of food and the defence against enemies.	Some fish school together for protection from predators.

Animals have special abilities that help them to live in a particular environment. Match the animal with its special ability.

kangaroo, cheetah, sperm whale, and cougar

Animal	Special ability	Advantage to the animal
1	Can hold its breath for over an hour	This ability lets it reach the bottom of the ocean to get food
2	Can jump high and broad and for long periods of time	This special ability helps them to get away from predators and to travel long distances
3	Can leap a long way	This helps it to catch its prey
4	The fastest land animal over a short distance	Short bursts of extreme speed allows it to surprise its prey

Try this

Animal reproduction

All living things have a limited lifespan, so they must reproduce to ensure their species continues to survive. Reproduction is the production of offspring.
All animals can increase their numbers but things like the availability of food and predators keep their numbers in check.
Animal reproduction follows one of two basic plans:

1. animals that can reproduce without having to mate (asexual reproduction)
2. animals that need two parents to mate and produce a fertilised egg (sexual reproduction).

All living things must reproduce to ensure their species continues to survive.

Asexual reproduction

Asexual reproduction is the form of reproduction that only needs one parent. Many simple animals reproduce without mating. Some just bud off small parts of themselves, whilst others develop from unfertilised eggs. Asexual reproduction is usually simple and fast and produces offspring with exactly the same blueprint or **genotype** as the parent. The offspring is therefore a **clone** with exactly the same genes as the parent.
The offspring grows up to have the same characteristics as the parent.

Sexual reproduction

Sexual reproduction always involves two parents who mate. The sex organs of each parent produce sex cells. When a male and a female sex cell connect, they form a fertilised egg called a **zygote**. This egg develops into a new individual, or offspring. The offspring has a unique collection of genes. These species have a better chance of survival because each offspring has a different genotype from both parents.

Example

Asexual reproduction is the form of reproduction that only needs one parent. Sexual reproduction always needs two parents. The other features of asexual and sexual reproduction are listed in the paragraphs above.

Try this

The table below compares sexual and asexual reproduction. Mark the correct box for each characteristic with a tick.

Characteristic	Asexual	Sexual
1 Involves mating		
2 Involves one parent		
3 Produces a zygote		
4 Different genotype from both parents		
5 Involves two parents		
6 Involves sex cells		
7 Has the same genotype as the parent		
8 Produces a clone		

ECOLOGY

The Earth is perfectly placed in the solar system to permit the existence and continued support of living organisms. It has large amounts of water, a good selection of gases, an appropriate temperature range, and suitable levels and types of radiation.

Environment

Ecology is the study of the relationships between living things and their environment. The natural environment of the planet includes the non-living things, or **abiotic** components (air, soil and water) as well as the living things, or **biotic** components. Flora is a term used to describe all the plant life of an area or the world. The fauna of an area consists of all the different kinds of animals found in the area. The **biosphere** encompasses every region of the Earth that is inhabited by living things.

Ecology is the study of the relationships between living things and their environment.

Ecosystems

Scientists divide the biosphere into smaller units called ecosystems, with particular sets of animals and plants. An ecosystem can be anything from a small puddle to a whole forest. Every ecosystem is made up of a **community** of living things and its surroundings.

Habitats

A small part of an ecosystem where the needs of a few species are met is called a **habitat**. There are many habitats within an ecosystem. A particular habitat usually has a predictable range of conditions such as food supply, temperature and rainfall. Some species are found in many different habitats and others may live in only a few. Examples of habitats are land, water, your backyard, local bushland, a stream or the soil. When a habitat changes, the needs of the living organisms may no longer be met.

Your backyard is a habitat for living things.

Niche

Living things have certain roles within the environment. An ecological niche is the precise way that an organism fits into its environment. The **niche** or role of an organism within the ecosystem is influenced by its habitat, its feeding habits and the temperature of the place.

Example

A backyard garden is an interesting ecosystem. It provides several habitats and the animals in each habitat fill different niches in each habitat. The compost heap in the drawing is just one habitat in this garden. It provides a home for woodlice, earthworms and millipedes. These animals feed on dead animal and plant material. Their niche or role in the garden is as detritus feeders.

Backyard Garden Ecosystem

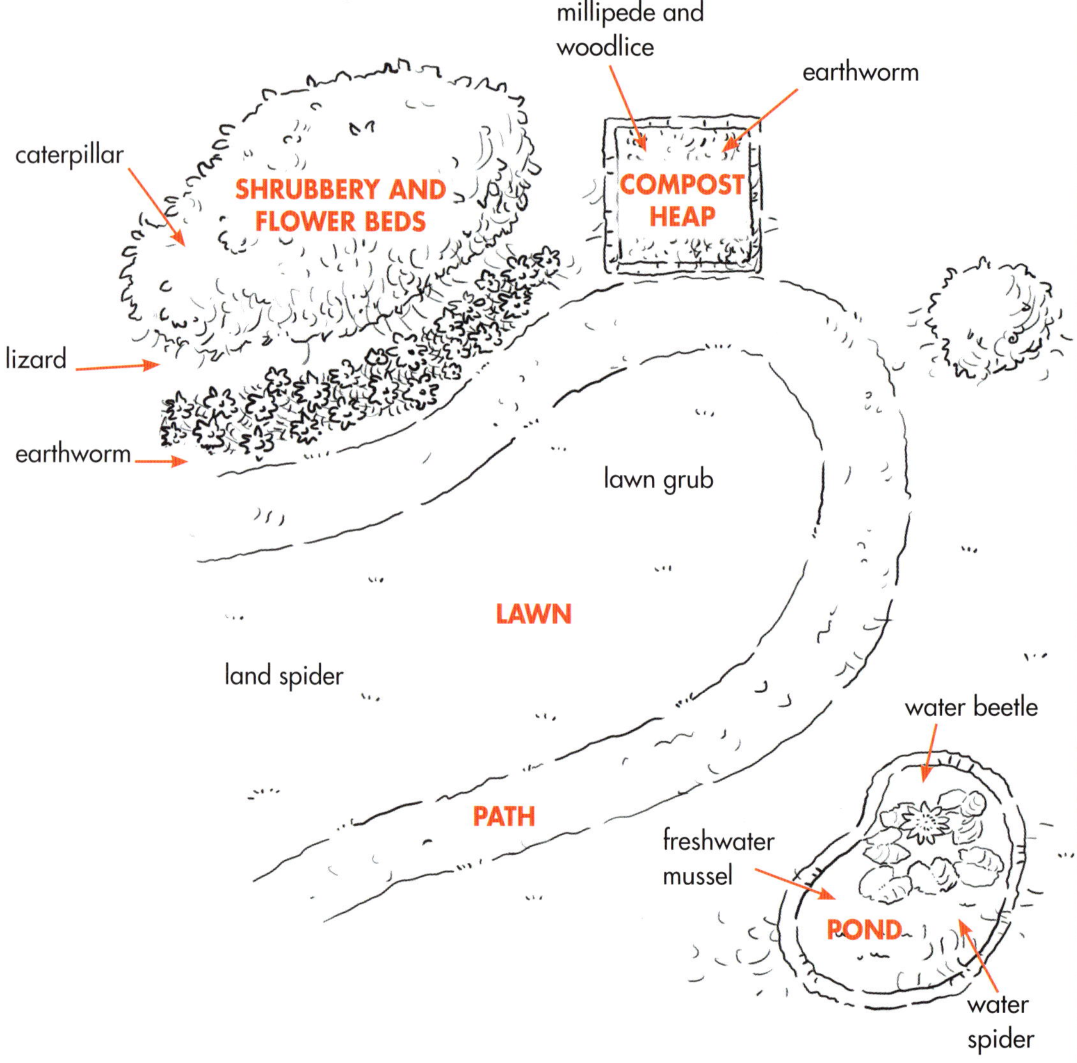

For the backyard garden shown above, answer the following questions.

1. Find three other habitats in this garden.
2. Which animals live in each habitat?
3. What niche does each animal fill in the habitat?

Flow of energy and matter in the natural world

Wherever you look the energy and the matter that we have here on Earth is always on the move.

Ecosystems and energy flow

Energy can pass:

- into and out of ecosystems
- from one ecosystem to another
- from one species to another within an ecosystem.

The flow of energy within an ecosystem is in one direction, from the sun and then from one organism to another along a food chain. The amount of energy passed on gets less at each stage or **trophic level**.

Food chains can be thought of as layers. The position each species holds in a chain is its trophic level.

Ecologists use **biomass** pyramids rather than pyramids based on numbers as they give a better picture of organic matter in an area.

Example

The diagram shows one food chain and three trophic levels – the plant, the wallaby and the dingo. Number pyramids show the actual number of animals in a food chain. Biomass pyramids show the mass of organic matter in a food chain. Energy pyramids show the amount of energy flow through a food chain.

plant (produces food) | wallaby (consumes food) | dingo (consumes food)

Which of the food pyramids below is a biomass pyramid that represents the above food chain? There are 100 plants (100kg), 200 wallabies (8kg) and 10 dingoes (1kg).

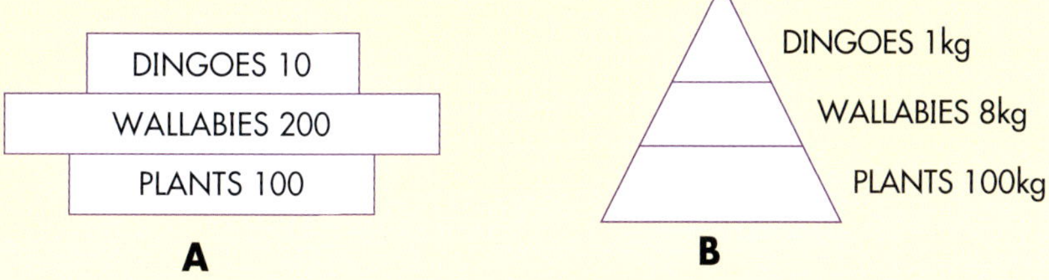

Try this

Ecosystems and the flow of food

Food chains and food webs show how food and energy pass between species in a community. A **food chain** is a pathway along which energy and nutrients are passed from one organism to another. **Food webs** are collections of interconnected food chains. The many different species in a community become involved in more than one food chain so a network is formed.

The following are the feeding processes in a food web.

- A **producer** uses energy to turn simple substances into food. A producer is the first level of a food chain. They make the food that supports the rest of the chain.
- A **consumer** is an organism that takes in food. There are many different consumers in a food chain.
- **Decomposers** break down the organic parts of dead things. They release raw materials, such as nutrients, minerals and carbon, back into the environment.
- A **parasite** lives on or in another species and feeds from that species (host). Liver fluke, pinworms and mistletoe are examples of parasites.
- A **predator** is a carnivorous organism that kills and eats others (prey). Predators have special **adaptations** to help them such as good vision, accurate sense of smell and strong legs for moving fast. Examples are leopards, eagles and dingoes.

A food chain is a pathway along which energy and nutrients are passed from one organism to another.

Symbiosis is a relationship between two different organisms where one or both benefit.

Example

The table provides an example for each of the feeding processes.

producer	consumer	decomposer	parasite	predator
plants	fungi insects rabbits possums foxes eagles	fungi bacteria	mistletoe tapeworms	eagles dingoes leopards

Study the collection of food chains in the food web shown.

1 What is the original source of food in the web?
2 How many food chains make up this food web?
3 How many trophic levels does the longest food chain have?
4 Which animals are carnivores and which are herbivores?

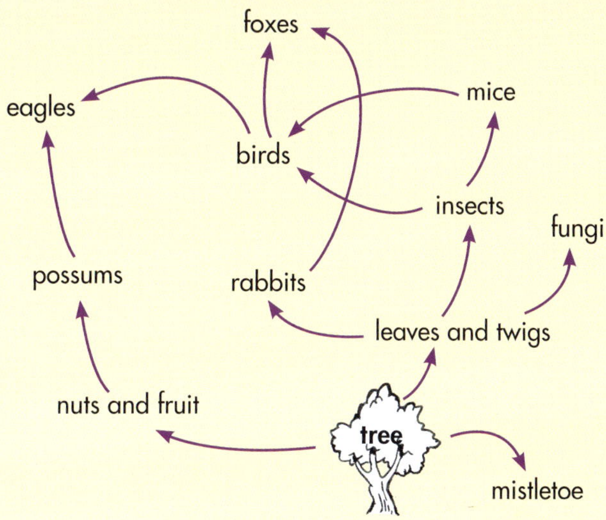

Try this

Ecosystems and the cycling of nutrients

Every ecosystem relies on the cycling of nutrients. Natural cycles ensure that there is no waste in nature and that the Earth's resources are continually reused. Some parts of a cycle can happen quickly, but others can last for thousands of years.

Nutrients

Elements essential to life, such as carbon, nitrogen and phosphorus, are returned to the ecosystem when living things die. Dead animals and plants are broken down by micro-organisms. These help to release all the nutrients and minerals in the organism back into the environment.

Example

Nitrogen cycle:

The atmosphere is about 80% nitrogen gas, but only bacteria can use nitrogen in this form. All other living things have to use compounds of nitrogen called nitrates. These are produced by the bacteria in soil.

The chemical, nitrogen, cycles from the atmosphere into the soil where bacteria produce nitrates. These nitrates are transferred to plants, then to animals and back to the atmosphere when organisms die and the nitrogen is released to the atmosphere through decomposition.

Carbon cycle: A large amount of carbon is locked away in the oceans, in fossil fuels and in plants. All living things contain carbon and this carbon is constantly recycled through the biosphere.

Place the following stages of the carbon cycle into the correct order. Start with A.

A A tree gathers sunlight and carbon dioxide, and produces food.
B Micro-organisms eat the tree and the vulture, releasing carbon back into the environment.
C The elephant releases the carbon that the tree gathered back into the environment as it decomposes.
D The elephant dies and a vulture eats the elephant.
E An elephant eats the leaves of the tree.
F The tree and the vulture die.

Survival and the interaction of living things

Living things depend on other living things for survival. Usually one organism will use another, but sometimes they work together to survive. Interactions between living things can be competitive or beneficial. Species may interact through feeding, shelter or reproductive needs such as pollination. If these links between species are compromised in any way, the ecosystem will become weaker.

Try this

Interconnectedness

A life cycle is the sequence of events that occur in the life of an animal or plant from its birth or germination to its death. Some life cycles last for only a few days (insects) and others for hundreds of years (a rainforest tree).

Example

The life cycles of plants and animals can be interrupted or weakened by environmental factors such as drought, fire, floods and disease. More or less of one species may cause an ecosystem to become unbalanced. If one species is able to dominate, then the ecosystem may collapse and another species may die out.

Refer to the food web on page 65.

1 What would happen if a disease killed most of the mice?
2 What would happen if a mouse plague occurred?

Adaptation

Through the process of evolution, living things become more suited to their way of life. They become better adapted to their environment by developing features that aid survival in an ever-changing environment. These features are inherited from one generation to another.

Example

There is a relationship between the position that leaves are found on a shrub and their shade of green. The leaves at the top of a shrub in full sunlight will be a lighter colour than those growing in the shade. The leaves in the sunlight need less chlorophyll to collect enough sunlight compared to those leaves in the shade.

Try this

What are the adaptations in each of the following examples?

A Parts of the Australian environment are very dry. Wattles have very hard seed coats to prevent the embryo from drying out. It takes a bushfire to weaken the coat so water can get in and trigger germination. Rain usually follows a bushfire.

B In high rainfall areas like rainforests, the leaves of plants have adaptations such as large holes to let rainfall through or spines and rolled tips to channel water off the leaf and prevent damage.

C Animals that live in Antarctica have adapted to the cold by developing thick layers of fat as insulation.

D Flowers that bloom at night are white and highly perfumed to be more attractive to moths as pollinators in the dark.

E Because they live in deserts, cactus plants have developed a large water storage capacity. They also have thorny spines to deter predators and aid survival.

Ecosystem balance

Ecosystems have evolved over time. Small changes to a system can be enough to alter its balance. Usually an ecosystem will overcome this imbalance. Severe natural changes caused by such events as cyclones, extended drought, fire and flood, will seriously affect the ecosystem. It may recover from these changes or may completely change. The growth and survival of living things are affected by the physical conditions of their environment. When a habitat changes, the needs of the living organisms may no longer be met.

Humans in the system

Human impact on the natural environment is wide reaching. Unlike animals and plants, humans exploit the environment for more than just food. Humans see a resource as anything in the environment that is useful such as energy, soil, coal, minerals, wood, plants, animals and water. Many civilisations have declined because they did not look after the environment.

Many civilisations have declined because they did not look after the environment.

Destroying habitat

- **Disappearing species**

  Each species is adapted to survive in its habitat. If we pollute or destroy that habitat, its plants and animals can no longer live there. Human activity has caused the extinction of 25% of animals and plants.

New houses for humans require the deforestation of bushland areas near cities using powerful machines. **What are the consequences to the fauna of such habitat destruction?**

Try this

Example

In Asia and in South America large areas of old tropical rainforest are still being logged. The fungus that some of the trees depend on is usually destroyed and without the fungus new trees cannot ever grow back. Fruit-eating bats and birds are deprived of their food sources and the whole forest suffers.

- **Pesticides**

  Humans use poisonous pesticides to kill the living things that they consider pests. Pesticides can spread everywhere and some last in the environment for many years. Pesticides build up in food chains and can be so high that those at the top of the food chain die of pesticide poisoning.

Example

If a fish eats thousands of tiny animals that have a small dose of pesticide in their bodies, the fish accumulates thousands of doses of pesticide in its body. With every fish that a water bird eats, the thousands of doses of pesticide are transferred to the bird. This process is called biomagnification.

Use the information in the bar chart to complete the following:

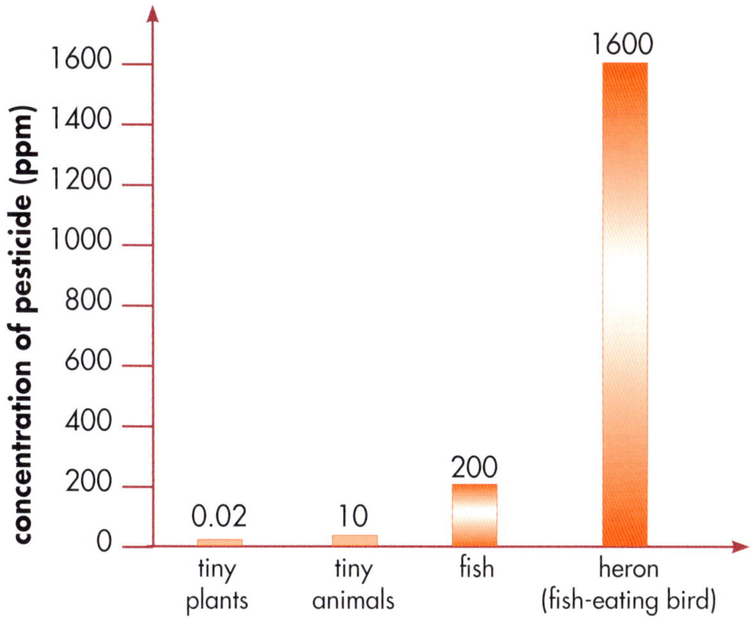

Food chain	tiny plants	tiny animals	fish	heron
Pesticide concentration (ppm)				

- **Global warming**
  During the 20th Century, the amount of carbon dioxide and other greenhouse gases in the atmosphere has increased. Scientists believe that this is partly due to deforestation and the burning of fossil fuels. The result has been an increase in the Earth's average temperature and if this continues, ecosystems may be compromised.

- **Oil spills**
  Oil spills from tankers and ships attract a lot of attention but they contribute only 10% of the oil that is polluting our water. More that 50% of the oil in the oceans comes from land-based sources such as leakage from industrial processes. However, it is mostly from people disposing of oil improperly and not recycling. The remaining oil gets into the water through ordinary marine operations such as cleaning on boats and ships at sea. Oil kills aquatic animals and plants.

PHYSICAL SCIENCES

Physical sciences develop knowledge and understanding of:
- **how an object's motion is influenced by a range of contact and non-contact forces**
- **how the concepts of force and motion apply to systems ranging in scale from atoms to the Universe**
- **how matter and energy react with each other**

Nothing in the Universe can happen without energy

ENERGY

Energy is defined by what is does, where it comes from and how it behaves.

What is energy?

Nobody really knows what energy is, so scientists describe energy by what it does. Energy makes things happen. Nothing in the Universe can happen without energy. Nothing happens when energy is just stored.

Matter is moving all around you and it takes energy to make it move. Things only happen when energy is transformed from one form to another, or transferred from one object to another.

Energy is invisible, responsible for all forces and measured in **joules** (J).

Where do we get energy from?

Most of our energy on Earth comes from the Sun and is stored in the Earth's matter. However, very little of the Sun's energy that falls on the Earth is used by humans directly.

Plants collect, process and store sunlight. Humans and other animals cannot do this. Humans and other animals need to wait for the energy to pass through a series of energy transfers. Sometimes it takes a few million years before energy appears in a form that we can use such as fossil fuels and food.

Renewable energy, such as tidal, solar, bio-fuel, wave and wind power, depends on the Sun's energy. Some energy sources that do not depend on the Sun are nuclear and geo-thermal sources.

How does energy behave?

Energy cannot ever be:

- used up
- created or destroyed, except in nuclear reactions.

Energy can be:

- stored
- transferred from one object to another object
- added to an object
- taken away from an object
- changed from one form of energy to another.

Example

Energy changes are happening in the following situations:

- *making toast – (electrical to heat)*
- *student riding a bicycle – (chemical to kinetic)*
- *wind farm – (kinetic to electrical)*
- *growing tree – (solar to stored)*
- *burning the tree – (stored to heat and light)*
- *petrol in a stationary car – (stored and no transfer until the engine is started then it is transferred to heat, sound and kinetic)*

Try this

Nine coins have been placed in a row on a smooth surface so that each coin is touching the next one. Another coin is placed about 12 cm from the back end of the row.

1 Predict what will happen if this coin is pushed quickly, so that it slides and hits the end of the row of coins.

2 Predict what will happen if a row of eight coins is hit with the remaining two coins.

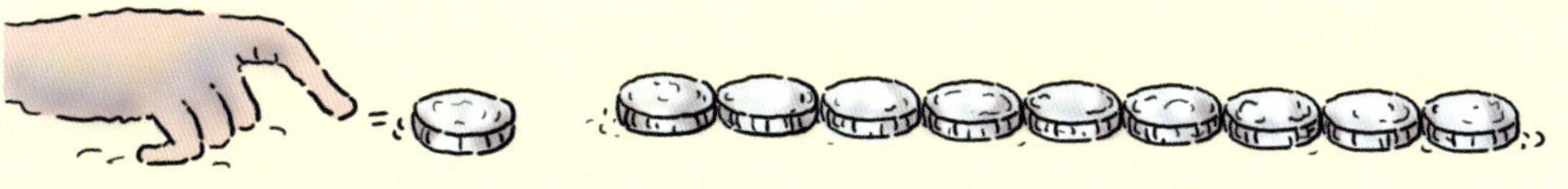

FORMS OF ENERGY

Forms of energy can be classified into two groups, potential energy and kinetic energy. Potential energy is stored energy. Kinetic energy is energy in action.

Potential energy

Potential energy is stored energy that is waiting to do something. The following forms of energy are some examples of potential energy.

Chemical energy

The energy stored in chemicals is often released when they are burned. Examples are food, wood and fossil fuels.

Elastic energy

Elastic energy is stored in matter that can be stretched, bent or compressed. For example, a set mousetrap, a stretched rubber band or a bouncing ball. The energy is released when the force holding it is released.

Example

A stretched trampoline demonstrates elastic energy.
A salad or a roast chicken meal is a source of chemical energy.
A person diving into a pool uses gravitational energy. An electric light bulb demonstrates electrical energy and a radio produces sound energy.

Gravitational energy

Gravitational energy is stored in an object when it is lifted above the surface of the Earth. If the object falls back to Earth, then this potential energy is released. For example, a trapeze artist has gained potential energy after climbing the ladder away from the pull of gravity. The potential energy is released when she falls onto the net.

Personal energy

Our bodies are like a machine. Each part needs energy to do its work. Chemicals called foods are eaten and the energy is released in our cells by a chemical reaction called respiration. This energy keeps us warm and allows hair, bones, muscles and skin to grow.
We also need energy for transport, comfort, convenience, housing and entertainment.

Nuclear energy

Nuclear energy is the energy stored in the **nucleus** of atoms. It can be released by **nuclear fission** from some atoms (uranium) in nuclear power plants. This energy can be used in the production of electrical energy.

However, the waste produced is **radioactive** and can kill living things. The **nuclear fusion** reactions in the Sun release vast amounts of energy providing us with heat and light.

Kinetic energy

Kinetic energy is energy that an object has when it is moving. A cyclist riding a bike has lots of kinetic energy. The kinetic energy in strong winds can cause a lot of damage but it can provide electrical power if harnessed.

Electrical energy

Electrical energy is carried by the **electrons** of atoms that push an **electric current** through a **conductor**. **Electricity** is mostly generated in power stations using fossil fuels or renewable sources. Electricity runs lights, computers, televisions, hair dryers and other equipment that requires energy in electrons.

Light energy

Light energy makes plants grow and burns your skin. It can be used to make a photograph. We can see because our eyes can detect light energy.

Heat or thermal energy

Heat or thermal energy is caused by the movement of the atoms in materials. It can cause one state of matter to change into another. We can sense heat with our skin. Heat can also cook our food and make water boil.

Sound energy

Sound energy is a special kind of kinetic energy. It is the energy of molecules as they vibrate. These vibrations are collected by our ears and processed by our brain.

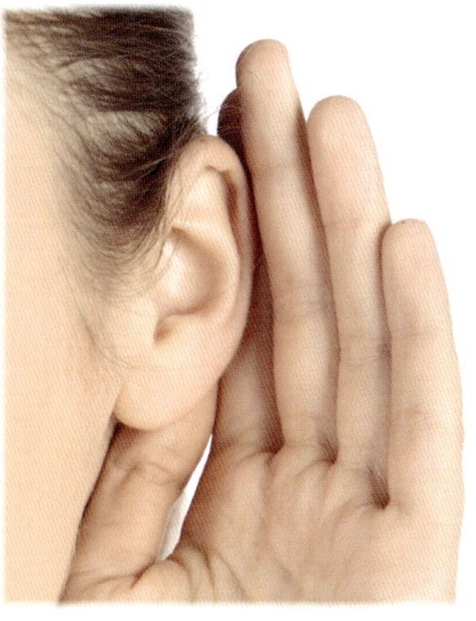

Use your knowledge of energy forms to explain what happens when you blow up a balloon with confetti inside it and then burst it with a pin.

HEAT ENERGY

Heat energy is caused by the movement of the atoms in materials.

What does 'hot' and 'cold' mean?

When matter is heated, its atoms **absorb** energy. The molecules of the matter vibrate faster and it becomes hotter. A substance is hot if its molecules have a lot of energy. The molecules of a cold object do not have as much energy. Its molecules vibrate slowly.

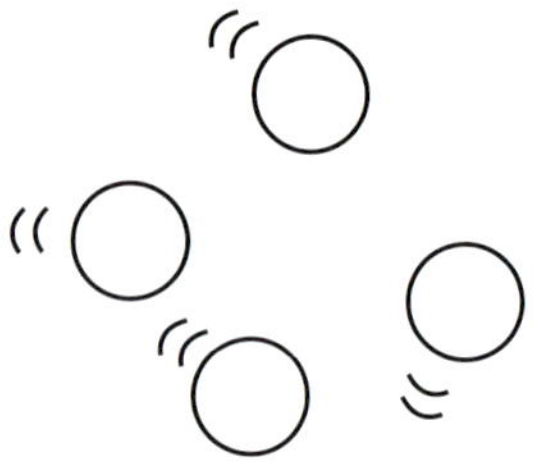

Cold molecules move slow

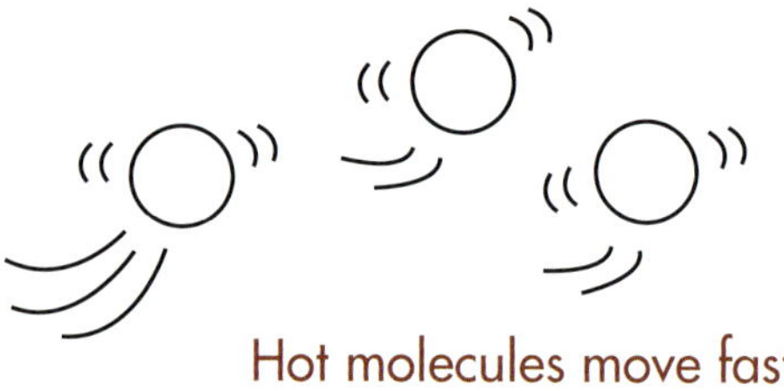

Hot molecules move fast

What is temperature?

Temperature is a measure of how hot or cold a substance is; not how much energy it has absorbed. Thermometers are used to measure temperature.

Thermometers are used to measure temperature

Heat transfer

Heat energy flows from the molecules of hot objects to the molecules of cold ones. Heat has only three ways to travel.

- **Conduction** is the movement of heat from molecule to molecule in a solid until the whole object is hot.
- **Convection** is the movement of heat from molecule to molecule in a liquid or a gas. The molecules in liquids and gases move faster, move apart and so take up more space as they absorb energy. A gas will rise as it becomes warmer. It is less dense and therefore lighter.
- **Radiation** is a special type of heat energy called electromagnetic energy, which does not need particles in order to travel. Radiation can therefore travel through a vacuum or through space. Radiant heat flows out from very hot objects such as the sun, a radiator or a fireplace. Dull black surfaces absorb radiation and shiny ones reflect it. Light, microwaves, infrared waves, radio waves and television waves are examples of radiation.

Example

Conduction is the movement of heat in a solid.
Convection is the movement of heat in a gas or a liquid.
Radiation is the movement of heat in vacuum.

Name the type of heat transfer that is occurring in each of the following.

A Heating water to boiling point in a kettle

B When holding a cup of hot chocolate, the heat energy is transferred from the hot chocolate, to the cup and then to your hands

C Feeling hot when lying on a beach in the sun

Conductors and insulators

Conductors transfer heat easily. Examples of conductors are metals and water.

Insulators transfer heat slowly or not at all. Examples of insulators are wood, styrofoam, plastics, newspaper and feathers. Insulators are used to keep hot things hot and cold things cold. Almost all insulators have air incorporated into them to make them more effective.

Example

Saucepans are made of metal because metal is a good conductor. Some saucepans also have copper bases and wooden handles. Copper is a very good conductor and efficiently transfers heat to the food, whilst wood is a good insulator and stays cool.

Try this

Predict in which order the paper clips will fall off. Explain your answer.

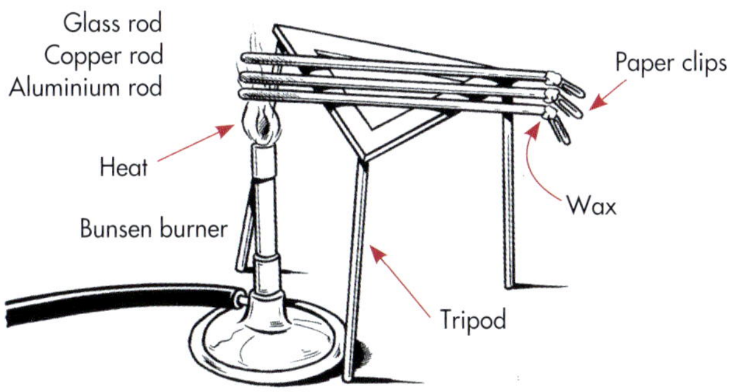

Controlling heat transfer

In our daily lives, there are objects that prevent heat transfer, so hot things remain hot and cold things remain cold. Wetsuits and thermos flasks prevent heat loss. White cars reflect heat.

Example

A fur coat is warmer if worn inside out, as it traps air close to the skin. This is like a bird that fluffs up its feathers on a cold day. In winter, a whale keeps warm by a layer of fat that is a good insulator. A thermos flask keeps things hot or cold depending on the temperature of its contents. The insulating effects of air bubbles in the rubber foam of wetsuits keep divers warmer.

1 What happens if you leave ice-cream at room temperature?
2 What would happen to ice-cream if you put it in the oven?
3 Study the method for making baked ice-cream.

Method: Ice-cream is put onto a sponge cake base and covered completely with a thick layer of beaten egg white and sugar, which when cooked is called meringue. The dessert is then baked in a very hot oven for 5 minutes. The meringue goes brown, the sponge cake gets warm and the ice-cream remains frozen.
Why doesn't the ice-cream melt?

Expansion and contraction

- When objects get hot, they get bigger – they expand.
- When objects get cold, they get smaller – they contract.
- When metals contract, large pulling forces are produced.
- When metals expand, large pushing forces are produced.

Try this

Example

A drinking glass will crack if you pour boiling water into it because the inside layer of glass tries to expand with the heat of the water but the outside layer stays the same temperature. The opposing forces cause the glass to crack.

1 Why are expansion gaps built into bridges, roads and railway lines?
2 Why are telegraph wires looped onto telegraph poles and not kept straight?
3 How does a thermometer work?

LIGHT ENERGY

Light comes mostly from the Sun and life without it would be impossible. Plants use sunlight to produce our food. Sunlight provides nearly all of our energy and warmth.

The distance light can travel through space in one year is a called a Light Year.

What is light?

Light is a form of energy that travels in all directions at very high speeds. Light rays travel in straight lines. If light rays hit something, they pass through (glass), bounce off (mirror) or are absorbed (bitumen).

Example

Light travels at a speed of about 300 000 kilometres in one second. It takes 8 minutes for the Sun's light to reach Earth.

Try this

Could the candle flame in the diagram be seen if the position of one of the cards is moved? Why?

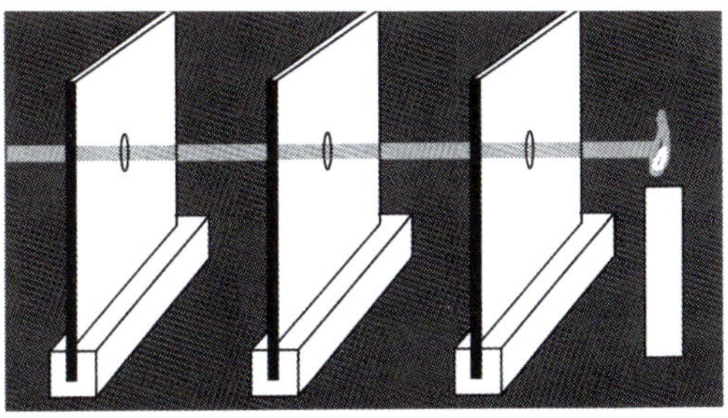

The colours of a rainbow are red, orange, yellow, green, blue, indigo and violet

What colour is light?

The light from the Sun is white. White light is not just one colour, but many colours mixed together. You can see these colours when raindrops bend the light and split it into the colours of a rainbow.

Different coloured objects absorb and **reflect** different amounts of each colour from the Sun's light. An object will appear whatever colour it reflects. All the other colours are absorbed. For example, a letterbox looks red because it reflects red light and absorbs the other colours. Some things are not coloured they are black or white. Black absorbs all the light, and white reflects all the light.

Blue light is reflected so the ball appears blue.

Example

A black car gets hot in the summer heat because it absorbs all the light energy. A white car stays cooler because it reflects all the light energy.

Try this

Study the diagram and label the arrow marked (A) with the correct colour. Explain your answer.

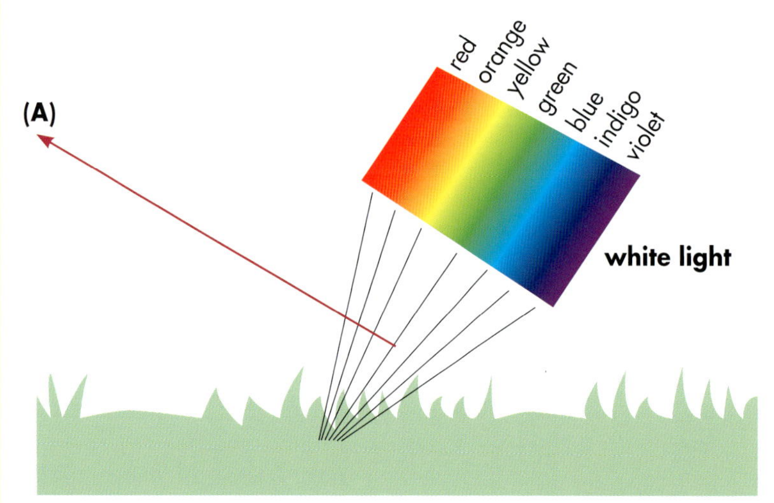

Sensing light

Our eyes can detect light allowing us to see objects around us. We cannot see things very well if it is dark, because there are little or no light rays to bounce off our surroundings and into our eyes. We can only see light if it bounces off an object.

- If an object is **transparent**, then the light rays pass right through it and we cannot see the light. For example, a glass window
- If an object is **opaque**, then some or all of the light bounces off the object and we can see the light and the object. For example, a chair
- If an object is **translucent**, then the object allows some light to pass through and some to be bounced off. For example, a frosted glass window
- Light bounces off in all different directions if the object has a rough surface and is not smooth.

We can only see light if it bounces off an object.

Shadows

A shadow is formed when light cannot pass through an object. Light spills around the object and creates an outline of the object's shape.
For example, an X-ray is a shadow, a sundial is a shadow clock and a lunar eclipse occurs when the Earth's shadow falls on the moon.

Example

Light will form a shadow when it hits a tree because a tree is opaque. All the light bounces off it and no light can pass through it so a shadow is formed.

Can you see a beam of light?

Try this

Reflection – bouncing light

Reflection occurs when a surface returns the light that hits it. Mirrors are very good reflectors as they are very smooth and the light bounces back following the same pathway. Mirrors are made of glass with a special reflective silver film on the back. Mirrors can also be curved.

Concave mirrors are used for car headlights to focus the light. **Convex** mirrors are placed on the blind corners of roads and in elevators to give a wide view.

Example

a rock
water
windows
cardboard
mirror
metal spoons
wood
stainless steel toaster

The highlighted objects are the best reflectors.
These objects have smooth, shiny surfaces. However, the mirror will provide the clearest image because the light bounces back at the same angle on the same pathway that it hits the mirror.

Try this

What sort of an image would you get from a fogged-up bathroom mirror? Why?

Refraction – bending light

Light changes direction or is bent when it moves from one material to another with different **densities**. This is called **refraction**.

Light travels *slower* in a denser substance, such as water, compared to a less dense substance, such as air, so it bends at the change in substance.

Light travels *faster* in a hot medium, so it bends when at the junction of hot and cold.
Refraction explains how a magnifying glass (convex lens) works and why mirages happen when air is very hot in some places and cooler in others.

Example

On a very hot day, aeroplanes appear to be landing on a runway covered in a shimmering pond of water because the air is very hot in some places and cooler in others. Light is refracted, or bent, causing an optical illusion.

Study the diagram and explain why the ruler bends.

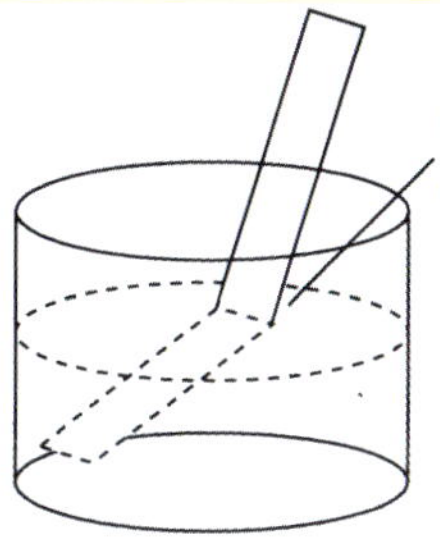

How we use light

Rainbows

White light is a mixture of many colours. When conditions are right, water droplets in the air can act as a lens or prism to separate the colours in sunlight – that is when you get a rainbow. Sometimes rainbows can be seen in fine sprays of water like a hose or sprinkler.

Primary colours

White light can be produced by mixing the appropriate intensities of the primary colours. These colours are red, green and blue, although any type of colour can be used. This mixing of the primary colours is used on television and computer screens to produce varying degrees of colour.

Stage lighting

People who work in the theatre use bright white spotlights and many coloured filters to set the mood on the stage. For example, yellow creates a happy or sunny mood and blue a cool one.

Optical instruments

Cameras, telescopes and binoculars use convex and concave lenses. Light enters the camera and passes through a lens that creates a small upside down image on a film. A simple refracting telescope has two lenses, and prism binoculars are made of two, tiny refracting telescopes side by side (one for each eye).

Periscope

While being submerged in the ocean depths, submariners can scan the surface of the seas, using the reflection of light from two mirrors at right angles.

Investigate the following colours of the Universe.

1. Why does the sky look blue from Earth?
2. Why does space look black from the Earth's moon?
3. What colour would the sky on Mars be during its day?
4. Why does the Sun look yellow?

Try this

Example

Sunsets and sunrises are so colourful because the Earth's atmosphere not only scatters light but it also bends it, separating it into lots of colours.

Diffraction gratings

A diffraction grating causes light to be refracted into different wavelengths. These help to make Australian bank notes one of the world's most difficult to counterfeit.

Fibre optics

Optical fibres are strands of glass or plastic that can carry light energy long distances. We can use light to send information around the Earth more efficiently than electrical energy. The telephone cables connecting the world are now made of glass instead of copper.

Synchotron

A synchotron is larger than a football field and makes super-bright beams of high-energy light.
Synchotrons are like sling shots for electrons as they shoot electrons at the speed of light. Scientists can learn about the sample under investigation by studying the patterns created by the light beams as they bounce off the sample.

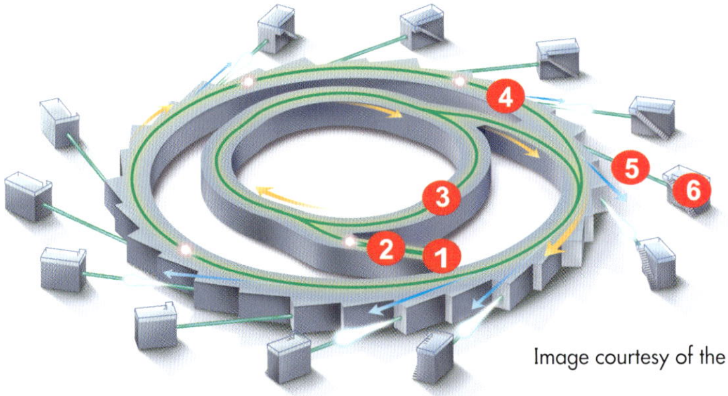

1 electron gun
2 linac
3 booster ring
4 storage ring
5 beamline
6 end station

Image courtesy of the Australian Synchotron

Laser

A laser produces a very powerful beam of light.
Lasers are used in surgery, by surveyors, in weapons and to measure very large distances.

SOUND ENERGY

Sound energy is a form of kinetic energy. It is the energy of molecules as they vibrate. Our ears detect these vibrations and our brain processes these vibrations so we can determine the sound – what it is? where does it come from?

What is sound?

Sounds are made by **vibrations**. The vibrations travel from one molecule to another, which results in a sound wave. We can see and hear these vibrations and they can bounce off reflecting surfaces.

Example

We can listen to the sounds of the world in terms of variations. Loud sounds vibrate back and forth through a larger distance than quiet sounds. This is called **amplitude**. *For example, when we can see a jet plane far away in the sky but still hear it. The sound of the jet plane is loud so it can travel longer distances.*

Try this

1. **Lie on the floor, eyes closed, be quiet and listen to the surrounding sounds.**
   What were the sounds?
   Were they loud or soft, high or low, long or short?
   What made these sounds?
   How do the sounds get to your ear?

2. **Put the palm of your hand on your throat and speak softly.**
   Describe what you feel.
   Try shouting, whispering, whistling, singing. Do you notice a difference in the vibrations?

3. Which has the largest amplitude, the sound of wind in the trees or the air brakes on a truck?

Sensing sound

Your ear is a structure that collects the energy in sound vibrations and transfers it to the brain. The brain interprets and processes the vibrations into sounds that we are able to understand. Sound is used by humans and other animals to locate objects and measure distance.

Example

We can hear insects, like mosquitoes and honey bees, because the flapping of their wings as they fly causes the air to vibrate.

A mosquito's wings beat at 300 times/second.

A bee's wings beat at 250 times/second.

Name an animal that has very large ears that can be rotated forwards and backwards to collect vibrating air from all angles. Can humans do this?

Try this

Can sound travel through a vacuum? Why?

How sound travels

Sound starts with a vibration caused by energy and radiates out from the source of the energy. The vibration is passed from one molecule to another as they bump around and a sound wave is produced. The energy received by each molecule is passed on, or transmitted but the molecule itself stays in the same place and vibrates back and forth.

Sound vibrations move through solids, liquids and gases but they cannot travel through empty space (vacuum).

Sound energy travels much slower than light energy. Sound travels at about 340 metres per second in air, about 1500 metres per second in water, and even faster in a solid. Light travels at 300 000 kilometres per second. Therefore, we see things long before we hear them.

Example

Sound travels faster through wood than air. Sound travels fast through wood because it is a solid and the molecules are close together. Sound travels slow through air as the molecules are far apart.

Musical sounds

Musical notes are produced by regular vibrations, such as the strings of a piano or the tube of air inside a trumpet or recorder. Different notes are produced by varying the size and speed of the vibrations.

Instruments that measure vibrations are called oscilloscopes

The number of vibrations in each second is called the **frequency**. Frequency is measured in **hertz** (Hz). For example, a guitar string that vibrates 196 times in one second has a frequency of 196 Hz. To produce vibrations with a higher frequency you need to tighten the string, shorten the string or use a thinner string.

Vibrations that have a high frequency (many complete to-and-fro movements per second) produce sounds that have a high **pitch**. The pitch of a sound is how high or low the sound is. It is determined by the length of the sound wave (**wavelength**).

The size of the vibration is referred to as amplitude. Amplitude determines how loud the sound is. A large amplitude produces a loud sound. Loudness, or the level of noise is measured in **decibels** (dB) using a sound meter.

Some objects collect and concentrate sound energy to make the sound louder – to amplify it. For example, your external ear, a stethoscope and a hearing aide are amplifiers.

Example

The diagram is a measure of sound waves.
The amplitude is the size of the vibration of the sound wave. The wavelength is the length of the wave.

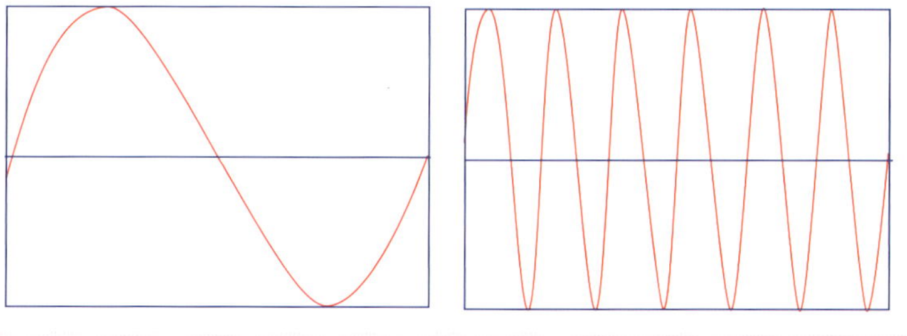

Complete the information below by using the words provided to fill in the gaps.

small, amplifiers, size, pitch, loudness, high, vibrations, soft, low, frequency, high

Like all wave motion, sound waves have length, amplitude and frequency. Amplitude is the ____ of the vibrations and determines _________. A _____ amplitude produces a ____ sound like a whisper. ________ is the number of vibrations per second and gives a sound a particular pitch. _____ can be high or low depending on the frequency of the ________. Rumbling thunder results from a ___ frequency and has a low pitch. A squeal has a ____ frequency and a ____ pitch. Musicians sometimes use __________ to concentrate sound energy and make the sound louder.

Try this

Sound and our world

Using sound to communicate

Grasshoppers make vibrations by rubbing parts of their bodies together. Mammals have vocal chords to produce vibrations. Humans are also able to formulate words to convey information and use tools such as the telephone and Morse code to communicate.

Nature's sound waves

- **Earthquakes**
  Seismic waves are the most devastating kind of sound waves. They cause seismic shaking, which is an earthquake.
- **Thunder**
  Lightning heats up the air by adding energy to the air particles. This causes the particles to vibrate and to move around taking up more space. These vibrations are called thunder. The faster the air expands the louder the thunder.
- **Heartbeat**
  You cannot hear a heartbeat but you can hear the vibrations produced by the valves in the heart when they open and slap shut.
- **Sound and health**
  People who listen to very loud music are damaging the structures in the ear that allow us to hear. These people may need hearing aids as they grow older.

Using the bounce in sound waves

- **Sonar**
  Sound **Na**vigation and **R**anging involves bouncing sound waves off an object and listening to the resultant echo. Ships use sonar to estimate the depth of oceans. Animals, like bats and dolphins, use sonar to find their way around and to find food.
- **Echoes**
  Echoes are heard if a sound bounces back from a reflecting surface. We hear the original sound more than once.
- **Acoustics**
  In concert halls, the acoustics depend on sound reflectors to bounce sound clearly from the stage to the audience.
- **Ultrasound**
  In medicine, an ultrasound bounces sound off internal body structures and these are recorded as pictures.

Example
Sound waves travel 1 kilometre in 3 seconds. If an echo is heard 6 seconds after making a noise, the reflecting surface is 2 kilometres away.

Try this

You see a flash of lightning and 4 seconds later, you hear the thunder. How far away is the storm?
(Clue: light travels at 330 m through air in one minute).

ELECTRICAL ENERGY

All matter is electrical. The atoms of matter are made up of small particles called electrons that carry a negative charge (-ve) and protons that carry a positive charge (+ve). Humans do not make electricity. We just need enough energy to make electrons flow through a conductor so producing an electric current.

Types of electricity

Static electricity

We cannot use static electricity to power electrical appliances because we cannot control the flow of electrons. However, if enough electrical charge builds up in the natural world, electrons will jump across a gap – we see this as a spark. Lightning is the transfer of electrons from clouds to other clouds or to the ground.

You can give an object an electric charge by rubbing it with a different material. For example, a plastic comb will become charged as it rubs against your hair. Two objects that have electric charges either attract or repel each other. Two positive or two negative charges repel, and a positive and a negative attract each other.

Current electricity

Current electricity will flow through wires to make an electric current. Since we can control this flow of electrons, we can make the electric current do lots of useful jobs. Electrons flow through conductors like copper very easily, but not so easily through insulators.

Electric current comes from the mains (you can plug into it, and turn it on) or from batteries (safest). To get an electric current from a battery you need to build a complete **circuit** with no gaps.

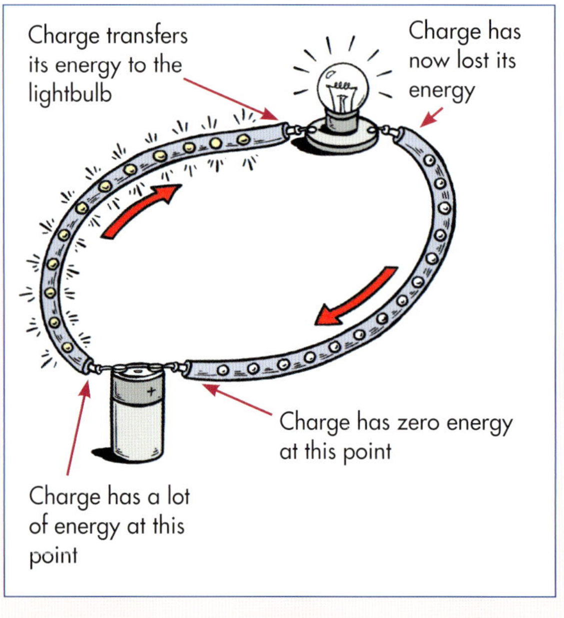

Example

The circuit diagram shows the current flow (arrows), battery, copper wires and bulb.

Study the circuit diagram on the preceeding page.

1 How do you know if an electric current is flowing through a circuit?
2 Would the current flow if the copper wire was changed to string?
3 What must you do to stop the electrons flowing?

Building circuits

Circuits provide a means of transferring and transforming electricity. Electrons can flow in an electric circuit only if the circuit is made of conductors. The simplest circuit is a bulb, a battery and some wires. If you add a switch, it is more useful.

A **switch** is a bridge for electrons. When the switch is open, no electrons can flow. When it is closed, it completes the circuit and electrons can flow. Insulators can be used to stop electrons going where they are not wanted such as plastic cabling around electric wires.

A **battery** provides the energy to separate electrons continually from **protons** and to push the electrons along the wire. It has positive and negative terminals.
A battery contains a paste, which is either acidic or basic, and two different metal connectors called **electrodes**.
A chemical reaction in the battery gives each electron some stored energy and electricity then flows from the negative electrode around the wires to the positive electrode.

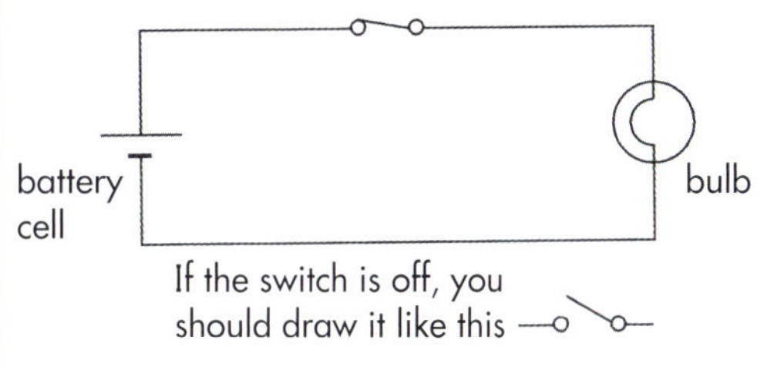

Wires in electric circuits are usually copper because electrons flow easily through it. The wires are connected to the **terminals** of a battery. If we add a second bulb to the circuit so that current flows through one bulb and then through the other bulb, then the bulbs are connected in order. They now share the current flowing in the wire so both lights are dimmer.

If we connect the two bulbs from the same battery but on different wires, then the bulbs are connected at the same time. Both bulbs are very bright because they are not sharing the electrons flowing in the wire; they have separate supply.

Circuits can be drawn using symbols.

A light bulb has a filament that gives out light when the electrons pass through it. If the filament breaks, the flow of electrons stops and the light goes out.

A fuse or a fuse wire is designed to break and stop the electron flow (current) if too much current is flowing. Too much current can cause a fire.

Electron flow in a circuit

1. Electrons from the negative terminal of the battery flow in one direction. The electrons carry energy along the wire until they encounter an appliance such as a buzzer or a bulb.
2. The energy carried by the electron is then transferred, for example, to a buzzer (sound energy) or to a bulb (light energy).
3. The electron then flows back to the positive terminal of the battery where it is given a new lot of energy and off it goes again.
4. If it cannot get back to the battery because there is a gap in the circuit, then everything stops until the circuit is complete again.

Example *Four circuit diagrams are shown. The circuit that correctly describes the electric current in the wires is circuit C. The current is flowing around the circuit in a continuous loop.*

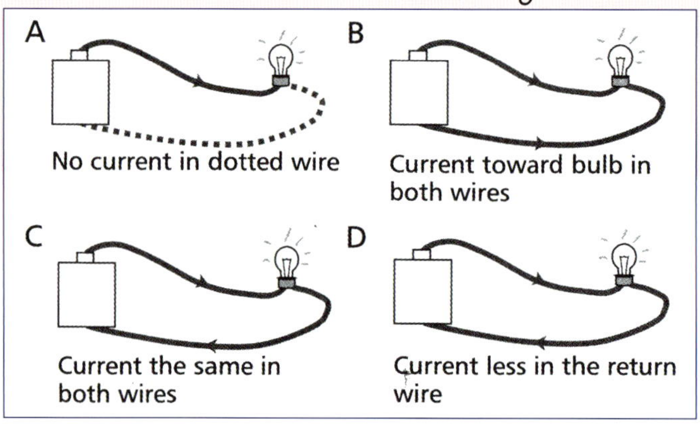

Try this

Look at the two circuit diagrams.

1. Which bulb/bulbs does the switch turn on in each case?
2. Which circuit, A or B, is connected up in parallel?

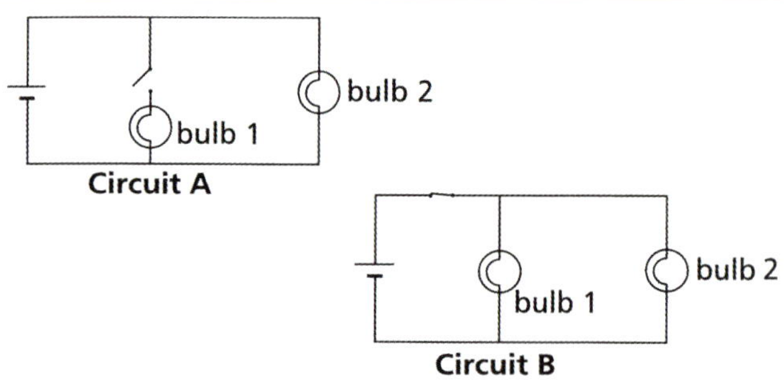

FORCE

Energy creates all forces. A force can be either a push or a pull. Forces make something happen. Forces can change the:

- speed of an object
- direction of movement of an object
- size or shape of an object.

A **force** is an action exerted upon an object, in order to change its state of rest or its state of motion in a straight line. Forces are measured in units called **newtons** (N) named after Sir Isaac Newton.

Newton's three laws explain what happens when objects move. **Weight** is the amount of pull that the force of **gravity** has on an object. The weight of an object depends on the mass of an object. **Mass** is the amount of matter (number of atoms) that makes up an object. Mass is measured in kilograms.

Balanced and unbalanced forces

A force does not always change the way something moves because a force may be balanced by another force. If an object is not moving, then the forces acting on it must be balanced.

For example, in a tug of war, if the rope was not moving and the teams remain in the same place, then the force exerted by both teams is equal so the forces are balanced.

Example

The whale in the diagram is basking in the sun.
The forces that are acting on the whale and allowing it to enjoy this activity are equal but opposite. The water is pushing upwards (upthrust) and balancing the downwards pull of gravity.

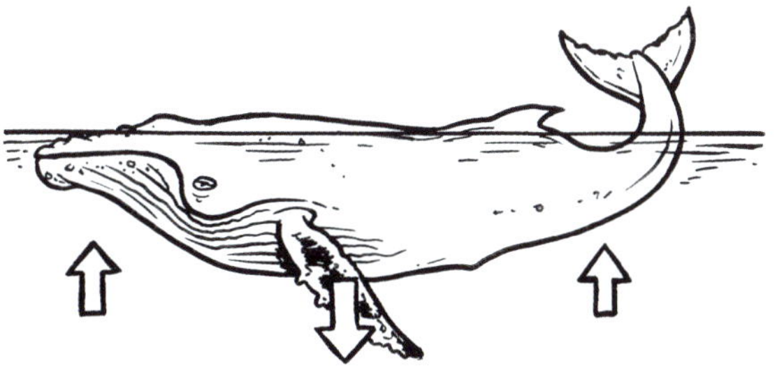

Read this information, study the diagram and then answer the questions.
Every airplane is in the centre of four forces – lift, thrust, gravity and drag. Lift and thrust must be stronger than the pull of gravity and drag, by just the right amount if a plane is to take off. Once an airplane is in flight it will continue to fly only if lift equals the pull of gravity and thrust is more than the drag of air resistance.

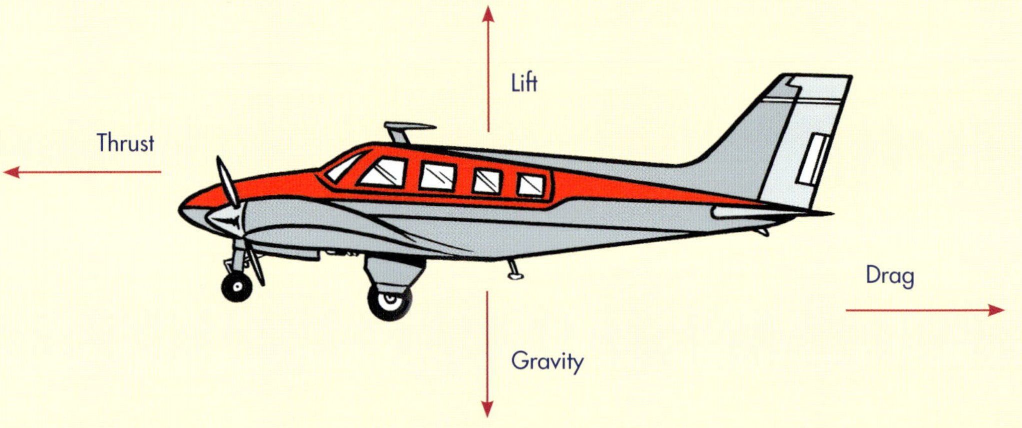

1 Match the force with the direction of its action.

force	direction of action
lift	forward push
thrust	air resistance (friction caused by air rubbing against the plane as it moves)
gravity	upward force
drag	weight

2 To be able to take off, these forces must be unbalanced.
Which two forces must be the strongest?

3 To remain flying once the plane is in the air:
Which two forces must remain balanced?
Which two must remain unbalanced?

Contact forces

Contact is a physical exertion of force. For example, a hand will exert a force on a door to close it. This type of force acts through direct physical contact.

Friction is a force that tries to slow down or stop the movement of an object. Friction is the force between two things rubbing together. It often makes things hot because some of the kinetic energy is converted into heat energy. This heat energy is usually wasted.

When an object moves through air molecules, the molecules rub on the object and this frictional force, termed **air resistance**, slows it down. When an object moves through a liquid, the liquid molecules rub against it and slow it down. This resistance to movement between solids, liquids and gases is called **drag**.

Friction is a constant force that opposes motion

Friction can be a nuisance in places where you want to go fast, such as snow skiing and bicycle racing. It is also troublesome where two surfaces rub so much that they wear away, such as the engine parts in a car.

The friction between moving objects can be reduced by:

- using a smooth surface
- lubricating surfaces with oil – moving parts in a machine
- separating the surfaces with air – hovercraft
- using wheels or rollers – moving heavy weights
- using streamlined shapes – rockets

Friction can also be very useful, for example, in the brakes of bicycles, tread on sports shoes, and the air friction in a parachute.

Example

This man on the tractor is trying to shift a log.
The force acting between the log and the ground is friction.
This force is acting in the opposite direction to the tractor – trying to slow it down.

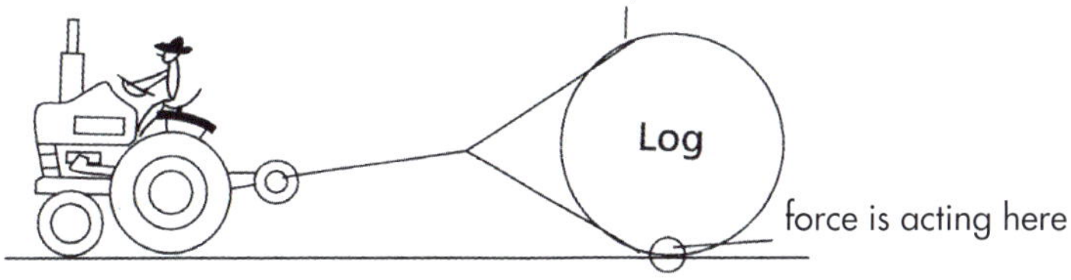

Look at the parachutist in the diagram and complete the sentence with the correct words: *gravity, decreases, increase, slows down, greater, gets faster*
(Note: two phrases too many have been provided)

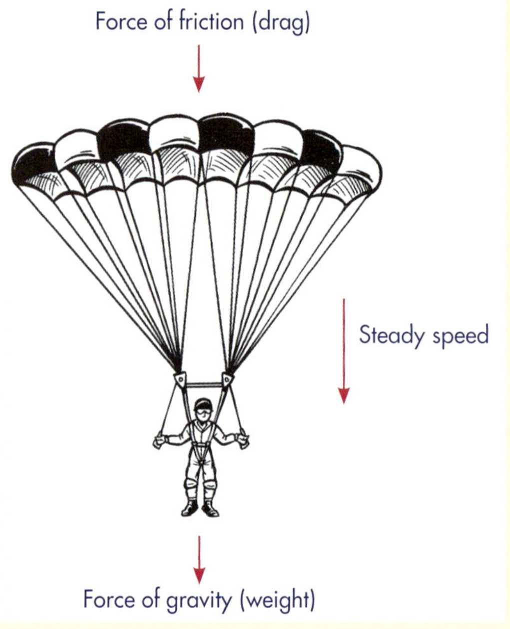

1 Opening a parachute ________ air resistance. If the air resistance is ________ than the ________ the parachutist ______________.
2 How does this parachutist make use of unbalanced forces?
3 Why does an object fall?

Try this

Non-contact forces

Invisible forces such as gravity and magnetism act without any direct physical contact.

Gravitational force

Gravity is the invisible force of attraction between all objects. Gravity holds the Universe together, keeps the planets in orbit around the Sun, helps keep satellites in their orbits and keeps us 'prisoners' on Earth.

Gravity depends on mass – the larger the mass, the larger the pull of gravity. It is small when it is between two people and very large between the Earth and the Moon. Gravity gets weaker the further from the Earth you are.

Gravity can only attract, it cannot repel. All of Earth's matter is governed by gravity. It pulls everything on or near it towards its centre and holds things there, even the atmosphere. The amount of gravitational force pulling on you can be measured. It is your weight.

Your **centre of gravity** is the point around which the weight of your body is centred. All objects have a centre of gravity. To stay balanced as you walk you need to keep your centre of gravity over, or between, your feet.

Energy can be used to create forces that will act against the pull of gravity

Example

If you jump high into the air, gravity will pull you back down to Earth again.

Eating and drinking depends on gravity to pull food down through your digestive tract – it is difficult to drink from a glass whilst standing on your head.

Try this

1. A yo-yo will always drop towards the centre of the Earth. How would you get this toy to work in zero gravity?
2. Can spiders spin webs in space?
3. Why do the roots of plants grow down and stems and leaves upwards?
4. A mouse could fall a 1000 m and not be hurt but a rat would be killed. Why?

Magnetic force

Energy gives us the forces that make things happen. Pulling and pushing are the two ways that energy can be applied as a force. Magnets push and pull.

Magnetism is an invisible force that attracts (pulls) or repels materials (pushes). The size of the magnet does not determine strength. Horseshoe magnets lift more than bar magnets. Gravity and electricity are also invisible forces.

Making magnets

Some materials are easily magnetised, for example, iron and steel. Iron is a magnetic material because it is easily made into a magnet by simply rubbing it with a permanent magnet. This action lines up all the atoms in a particular order. If the new magnet is dropped, the atoms will become mixed up again and the magnetism is lost.

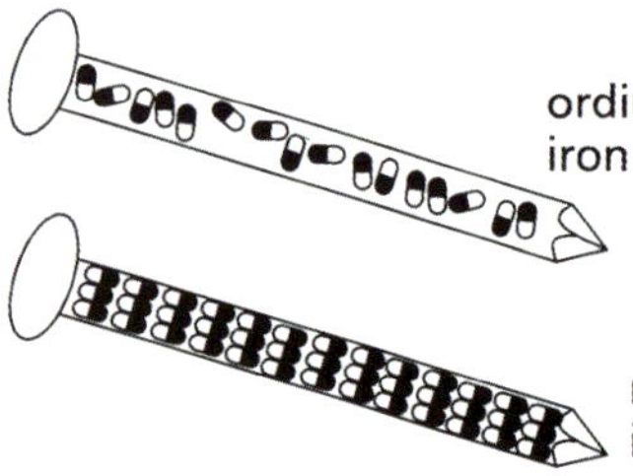

A **magnetic field** is the space around a magnet. This is the area where one object can exert a magnetic force on another without actually touching. The field gets weaker as the distance from the magnet increases. All magnetic substances can produce magnetic fields that **attract** or **repel**.

No matter what shape a magnet is, it always has two **poles** – a north pole and a south pole. The pole of a magnet is where the magnetic force is strongest. Different shaped magnets all have poles (the poles of a donut shaped magnet are on the top and bottom surfaces). Just like static electricity, like poles repel and unlike poles attract – so two north poles will repel but a north and a south will attract. The magnetic field can be mapped by using iron filings, which line up along the lines of force.

A magnet moving something is a magnet at work

The Earth is a giant magnet with both a north and a south pole. All magnets are affected by the Earth.

Example

The following magnets show the position of the poles and the direction of the force fields.

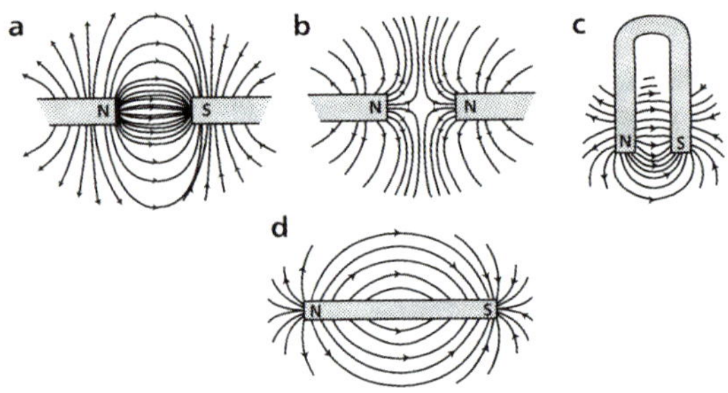

Try this

The magnets in this diagram are 'floating' – if you try to push them down, they repel each other. Explain how this works.

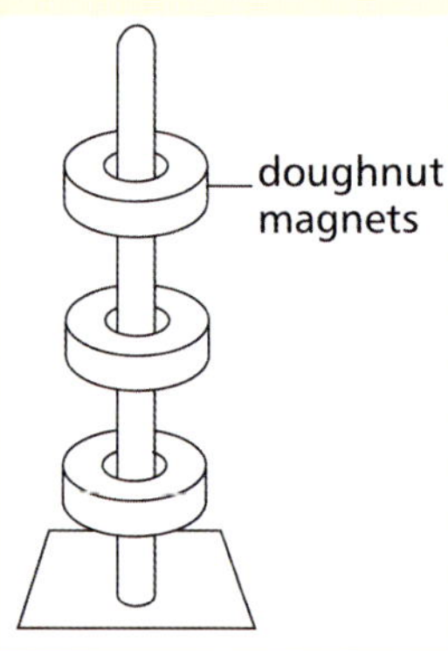

MOTION

Sir Isaac Newton (1643–1727), was an English scientist and mathematician. Newton's three laws have given scientists an understanding of the way that force and motion are related. The laws have always seemed to explain every movement in the Universe perfectly. Physicists are now finding even deeper understandings of force and motion.

Newton's first law of motion

Things like to keep on doing what they are already doing. They do not like to start moving or stop moving – they are 'lazy' – they have **inertia**. Inertia is an invisible force and can be defined as 'difficulty to move'. The larger the mass of an object the larger the force needed to get it moving.

Moving objects also need a force to stop them moving, as their inertia tends to keep them moving in the same direction. Every object stays at rest or moves at a constant speed in a straight line unless a force acts on it. If the forces on an object are balanced then:

- if it is at rest, it stays at rest
- if it is moving, it keeps moving at a constant speed in a straight line.

Example

Imagine an orange placed on a table. According to Newton's first law, the orange will stay there forever and would only move if a force were added to it.

Try this

In terms of Newton's first law, what is happening in the drawing?

Turning forces

Some objects will not move along because they are fixed at a point, but they may move around this central point. If you whirl a cork on a piece of string, around your head, you can feel the force in the string.

Newton's first law says that the cork will continue to move in a straight line unless a force is applied. This force is your hand pulling on the string. This force is acting towards the centre of the circle and keeps the cork from going straight ahead. This force is called centripetal force and the cork moves in a circle.

The Italian scientist Galileo (1564–1642) laid down the groundwork for Newton

Newton's second law of motion

If you want to move an object to another place, you will have to add a force. Two things about this force are important: the size of the force and the direction of the force.

Because size and direction are important, force is called a **vector quantity**. Vector quantities have both direction and magnitude (size). **Velocity** and **acceleration** are both vector quantities.

Resultant forces

Vector quantities, like forces, can be added. If two forces of 2 newtons each are acting in the same direction, the **resultant force** is 4 newtons in one direction. If they were acting in opposite directions, then they would cancel out and nothing would happen.

Velocity

Velocity is almost the same as speed but it is a vector quantity so it has size (speed) and direction.

Would a spacecraft moving through space in the absence of any forces have a constant velocity?

Try this

Example

If a bicycle is moving at a steady speed of 10 metres every second, it is not changing – it has a constant speed. If it is moving at a constant speed in a straight line, it has **constant velocity**.

Acceleration

Acceleration is just a change in velocity. If the person on the bicycle pedals faster, the bicycle goes faster – it accelerates. If the bicycle accelerates, then the velocity increases.

Newton's second law of motion states that when an unbalanced force acts on an object it accelerates in the same direction as the force.

The law is about how a force affects the movement of an object. The greater the force on an object, the greater is its change in speed or direction. The heavier an object, the less is its change in speed or direction.

Force (N) = mass (kg) x acceleration (m/s/s) [measured in newtons (N)]

Example

1 N is the force that gives a mass of 1 kg an acceleration of 1 m/s/s.

What is the force of gravity on a 1 kg mass if the acceleration is 9.8 m/s/s?

Newton's third law of motion

This law describes the effect of interactions between two objects. For example, friction is a force that tries to stop motion happening.

Newton observed that forces are always in pairs but opposite in direction. He called the two forces action and reaction. Newton's third law is for every action there is an equal and opposite reaction.

The action force and the reaction force are equal and opposite. Some other things that work this way are cannons, jet engines, squid propulsion, turning the hose on without holding it and explosions. The forces are equal but opposite.

Example

If you rest your elbow on a table, the forces on your elbow are equal and opposite. The downwards force of your elbow on the table equals the upwards force of the table on your elbow.

Try this

As the fuel inside a space craft burns, hot gases expand and then rush from the rocket at tremendous speed through the exhaust nozzle. How does Newton's third law apply to this situation?

CHEMICAL SCIENCES

Chemical sciences develop knowledge and understanding about the composition and behaviour of substances.

Atoms are the smallest pieces of a substance

WHAT ARE MATERIALS?

All the materials of Earth, such as plastic, wood and rock, are made of **atoms**, with empty space between them. Atoms are the smallest pieces of a substance. The smallest bunch of atoms is called a **molecule**. Scientists call bunches of molecules matter. A material can be made of the same kind of atoms or a mixture of different atoms. A bunch of atoms can be broken up and re-mixed to make different materials.

What is matter?

The Universe is made up of atoms, the energy they contain and the space between them. There are about 107 different types of atoms on Earth. Scientists list these in a table called the **Periodic Table of Elements** (atoms).

Example

Can you see some matter? Maybe you can see carpet, hair, shoes, jewellery.
Use your senses to describe a piece of matter.
Is it rough, hard, smooth, small, colourful, will it balance on one finger? What is your matter made of?
It will be made of a mixture of tiny particles that scientists call atoms. We cannot see atoms because they are too small, even for our biggest microscope.

Try this

1. Is there anything in the Universe that is not matter?
2. How many different kinds of atoms do we have on Earth?
3. Can you name some materials that are made mostly out of carbon atoms? Wood and diamonds have carbon atoms.
4. Can you name some materials that are made mostly out of aluminium atoms?
5. Can you name a material that is made mostly out of hydrogen and oxygen atoms joined together? (Hint: It covers about 70% of the Earth's surface)

Characteristics of matter

- We cannot create new matter and we cannot destroy matter, but atoms can be re-arranged.
- The amount of matter (atoms) in a substance is called its **mass**. Because matter is just lots of atoms it can be weighed.
- If atoms are packed very tightly together they have more mass (a greater number of atoms in a given space) and therefore weigh more. They are said to be **dense**.

Example

Materials such as lead sinkers are very dense and weigh a lot compared to a marshmallow which is mostly air with only a few atoms. Gases like the atmosphere are even less dense and do not weigh much at all.

Compare rice bubbles and butter and then answer the following questions.

1. Which do you think will weigh the most – a kilogram of rice bubbles or a kilogram of butter?
2. If a kilogram, butter container is filled with rice bubbles and compared with a kilogram of butter, which will weigh more? Why?
3. Why do you think it is easier to throw a light rock further than a heavy rock?

Try this

Tightly packed atoms have more mass

atoms of a gas

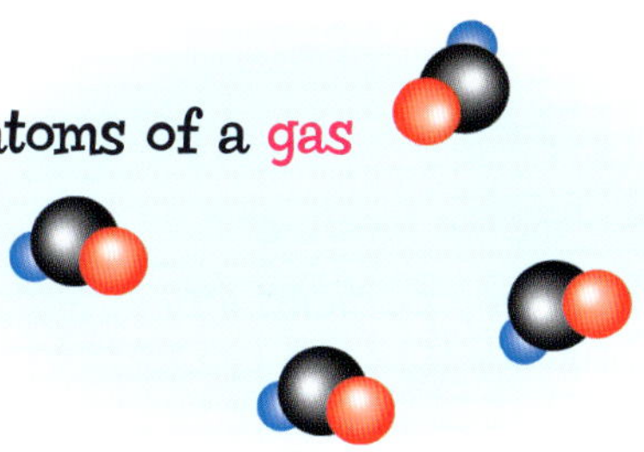

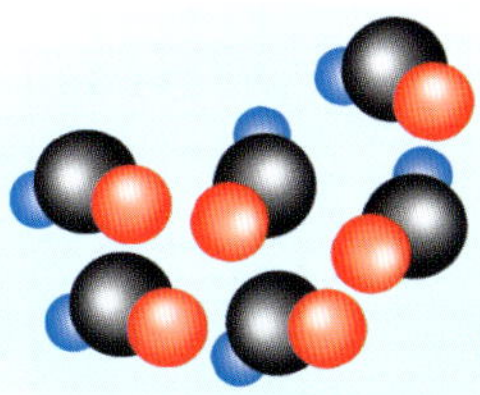

atoms of a liquid

atoms of a solid

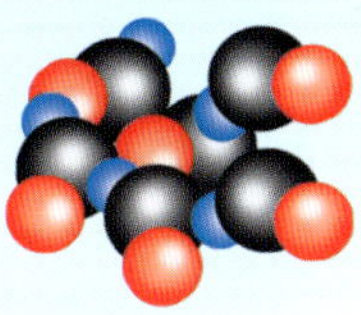

CLASSIFYING MATERIALS

Substances or materials can be grouped according to:

- their composition (**elements**, **compounds** or mixtures)
- their **properties** (solids, liquids or gases).

Mixtures

Most substances and materials in industry and in nature are mixtures. The atoms in a mixture can be totally muddled up like marbles in a jar.

We can use the properties of materials to separate **mixtures** made of several substances. By using one or more separating techniques, we end up with **pure substances** that cannot be separated out into components.

Sieving, filtering, floating and evaporation are examples of these separating techniques.

The main types of mixtures are:

- A **soluble** solid dissolved in a liquid (for example sugar in water). This mixture is called a **solution**.
- An **insoluble** solid suspended in a liquid (for example mud in water). This mixture is called a **suspension**.
- One soluble liquid dissolved in another liquid (for example oil and petrol make 2-stroke mower fuel). This mixture is called a **solution**.
- One insoluble liquid suspended as droplets in another liquid (for example oil and vinegar in a salad dressing). This type of mixture is called an **emulsion**.
- Grains of different solids mixed together (for example salt and pepper).

Example

The sand from a suspension of sand in water can be recovered by evaporating the water off. Cooked spaghetti can be separated from the cooking liquid by sieving.

Soft drink is a mixture of water, sugar, carbon dioxide, food colouring and flavours.

1 What kind of mixture is the drink?
2 When we release the lid, what is separated from the mixture?

Pure substances

Pure substances always behave in the same way. For example, they have constant melting and boiling points. There are two types of pure substance:

Compounds and elements are pure substances

1 **Compounds** can be decomposed, by such things as heating, to form simpler pure substances or elements.
   Compound + strong heat →2 (or more) elements
2 **Elements** cannot be decomposed no matter what we do to them. They can however combine chemically to form compounds.
   Element (x) + Element (y) →Compound (z)

Example

Some common pure substances include table salt, water, copper, diamond and oxygen.

*The **elements** in this group are copper, diamond (carbon) and oxygen.*

*The **compounds** in this group are table salt (sodium and chloride), and water (hydrogen and oxygen).*

Classify the following as elements, compounds or mixtures

silver pendant, confetti, aluminium foil, fruit cake, sugar

THE 'STATES OF MATTER'

On Earth we are just far enough away from the Sun's energy so that matter can be in a solid, liquid or gas state. Scientists call these three states the 'states of matter'.

The states of matter: solid, liquid or gas

Heat energy can cause one state of matter to change to another state such as adding heat energy to water changes it to a gas (water vapour change). The only difference between them is how much energy they contain.

A **solid** is something that maintains its shape.
A **liquid** maintains its volume but takes the shape of the container. A **gas** has no fixed volume, but does take up the volume of its container. The state of matter depends on both the matter itself and the temperature.

Example
The energy removing machine in your kitchen is a fridge or a freezer.

Try this

1 What happens if you add lots of energy to water (liquid)?
2 What happens if you take this energy away again?
3 What happens if you take even more energy away?
4 How could we reverse this process?

Solids, liquids and gases

Materials behave differently depending on their state and are therefore used for different purposes.

- The molecules of a **solid** are packed closely and neatly together and are not free to move around.
- The molecules of a **liquid** have marginally more space between the molecules and can roam around, rolling and sliding over one another.
- The molecules of a **gas** are far apart, have lots of space between them and are free to zip around all over the place.

Example

Look at the three closed bottles with water molecules trapped inside. Bottle A contains the most molecules. The molecules in the solid are not moving, in the liquid they are moving a bit and in the gas they are zipping all over the place. The molecules of a solid or a liquid cannot be forced together because there is no space between their molecules. However, the molecules of the gas can be compressed quite easily.

A. Solid molecules **B.** Liquid molecules **C.** Gas molecules

Try this

Study diagrams A and B.

A.

B.

1 Explain diagram A.
2 Can a person really run through a fence? Explain your answer.
3 Can you run through a gas?
4 Would a gas make a very good fence?

Combining the states of matter

A balloon is a stretchy skin inside which we trap air.
A bubble is the same.
These elastic skins hold the gas in place.

A foam is a substance that is formed by trapping many bubbles of air in a liquid or a solid.
To stabilise the surface of the bubbles, as well as hold them in place, another substance must be added.

Example

Bubbles in water do not last very long but if detergent is added, bubbles last much longer. Soft drink also makes lots of foam as dissolved substances in the soda stabilise the bubbles making them last longer.

Try this

There is a well known drink called the 'Ice-cream Soda'. It is made by pouring a soda drink over a scoop of ice-cream. Lots of foam is produced, which lasts quite a long time making it fun to drink.

1. How does ice-cream help with foam production?
2. Can you think of any other examples of foam materials?

CHANGING MATERIALS

Materials can be changed by either their physical or chemical state.

Physical change

A **physical change** in a material involves a change in its physical state (solid, liquid, gas) or in its appearance. Physical changes are usually easy to reverse.

Examples of physical changes are:

- Adding heat energy to:
  - melt a solid into a liquid
  - boil a liquid into a gas.
- Dissolving a substance in a liquid to make a solution.
- Rolling a block of metal into sheets, drawing it into wires or grinding it into a powder.

Example

Add heat to chocolate and it melts to become a liquid.
Stir sugar into a hot cup of tea and it dissolves.
Grind chalk and it becomes a powder.
Force plastic through little holes and it makes nylon fibre.

Try this

Describe how you would reverse the physical changes in each example above.

Water does not obey the rules

Adding energy to a material causes the atoms to move faster, to move further away from each other and take up more space. If we take energy away, the atoms usually move slower, move closer together and take up less space. Water does not obey these rules. When energy is removed from water, it becomes ice. The ice should take up less space. But it actually takes up more space because the molecules form the geometric pattern of a **crystal**.

Example

Have you noticed what happens if you accidently freeze a whole bottle or can of soft drink in the freezer? The soft drink is mostly water, and water takes up more space when it freezes so the can or the bottle splits or bursts open.

Try this

Why is there a 'dint' or depression in the side of a two-litre plastic milk bottle?

Chemical change

Sometimes when pure substances are mixed, or a single substance is heated, new substances are formed. Such changes are called chemical changes or **chemical reactions**. When substances rearrange their atoms between the molecules to give different chemical substances, a chemical reaction has taken place. Two examples of chemical reactions are **combustion** and corrosion (rusting).

Example

When we burn wood (combustion), each carbon atom in the wood combines with an oxygen molecule (two oxygen atoms) to form carbon dioxide. Because the atoms are now joined together differently, carbon dioxide has different properties from those of either oxygen or carbon.

Corrosion is the reaction of a metal with another element, usually oxygen, in moist air to form a new substance.
Iron + oxygen–> iron oxide (rust)

Try this

Look at the diagram and answer the questions.

1. Which nail do you think would rust?
2. What is the name of the chemical reaction that is occurring in this test tube?
3. What element is the iron combining with?
4. Why was oil put on top of the water in tube A?

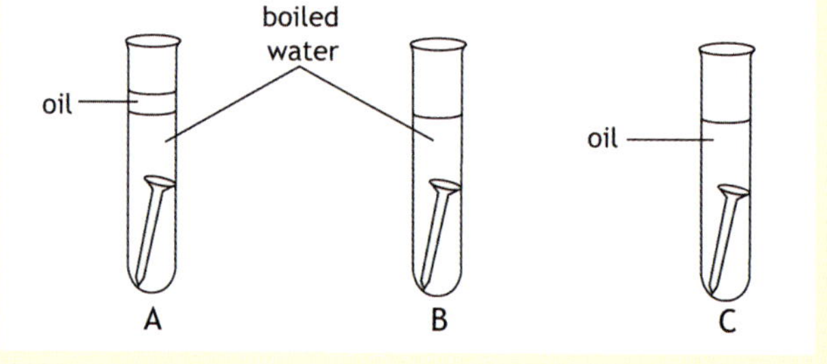

Note: Boiled water contains no air (oxygen) and air (oxygen) cannot penetrate oil.

PROPERTIES OF MATERIALS

There is a relationship between the way atoms are arranged in a substance and the way that the substance behaves. For example, a graphite pencil and a diamond are both made of carbon. The carbon atoms are arranged differently in the diamond, which makes it hard, shiny and brilliant instead of dark and soft like the graphite pencil.

Different materials have different properties, so we can use them for different purposes. For example, steel is strong, rubber is flexible and glass is transparent. These different properties influence and also limit the materials use. The properties of materials determine how new materials are developed for new purposes and how new roles are found for existing materials.

Example

Think of a car. What types of materials are used to make a car? Glass is used for the windows because it is transparent. The chassis is made of steel for strength. Tyres are made of rubber because it is tough, flexible and can be moulded to hold air under pressure.

Many materials around us are solids. Some are harder than others, some are very flexible and others snap or bend easily. The way that particles are arranged in a solid can make a big difference to such properties as hardness, flexibility and melting.

1 Which of the following materials is able to bend without breaking?
glass, piece of fabric, chalk, paper, plastic sheeting, metal, wooden pencil, wire

2 Why would it be a bad idea to construct a building out of chalk?

Natural materials

Many plants and animals build structures in the natural world. We only have to think of enormous rainforest trees, termite mounds, bird nests and the Great Barrier Reef. Many of these structures are very strong and incredibly complicated.

Example

Some of nature's materials are stone, wood, gems, cane, cotton and gold.

Match the examples of nature's structures with the description.

Structures – *honeycomb, tree, bones, bat's wings, spider web*

Structure	Description
	We hang all our squishy bits (organs) onto these.
	This is an extremely strong material, used to trap squirming insects for food.
	This material is elastic and when stretched over bone it is designed to catch the wind.
	The trunk supports branches, leaves, fruit and flowers and bends or deflects when resisting strong winds.
	This structure is made of wax to store honey – wax is not a strong material but the hexagonal shape makes a very strong structure.

Processed materials

Humans have worked out how to make useful materials using the natural substances found on Earth (resources). Some examples are plastics, soap and detergents, glass, paint, paper and glues.

We can make plastic from natural substances like milk, cotton or wood. However, most of our plastics are made from coal or oil. There are many different plastics and they do not all behave the same way. Chemists have designed plastics to behave in different ways, to have different properties, so that we may use them for different jobs.

Example

Some plastics will melt (straws), others will just soften (takeaway cups) and others will burn if exposed to the heat of a flame (disposable cutlery). Some are biodegradable (made from natural products) and some are not (some supermarket bags). Some plastics will stretch and others will shrink. Some plastics float in water and some sink. When some plastics are heated, the plastic shrinks and sticks together. When the plastic is cooled again, it forms a seal.

Try this

Some students were investigating the properties of plastics. They put a potato chips packet and a soft drink bottle into an oven. When the objects were removed from the oven, they were only a quarter of the original size.

1. What property was demonstrated in this experiment?
2. What is this property of plastics used for?

Choosing and using materials

We should consider the following questions when choosing a material for a certain purpose:

- What are the materials properties? (how it behaves)
- Is the material strong enough?
- Does the material need to be light or heavy?
- Can we change the shape of the material to suit our needs?
- Will the material last long enough or will it break or rust?
- Can we get enough of this material?
- How much will the material cost?

The 'Three Little Pigs' is a story about choosing and using the best materials for the job.

Strength of materials

Some materials have **strength**. The strength of a material is how much force a material can stand before it breaks. Some materials are strong and some are weak. Different shapes of the same materials have different strengths. Triangular and cylindrical shapes are strong.

Methods and materials used to join the parts of structures must provide strong but flexible connections such as the stitching and glue used to join the pages of a book.

Example

Paper is strengthened to do particular jobs. Examples of strengthened paper are thick and thin cardboard, corrugated cardboard. Some objects made from strengthened paper are toilet roll tubes and cardboard boxes.

Try this

Students designed a paper bag using two double sheets of newspaper and 20 centimetres of masking tape and two paper clips. The bag had to be strong enough to carry two kilograms of potatoes a distance of 10 metres. The handle could be separate or part of the bag.
Study the bag made by the students.

1 When strength was required, what things did the students do to the paper to make it stronger?

2 What was the weakest part of their bag? How could it have been made stronger?

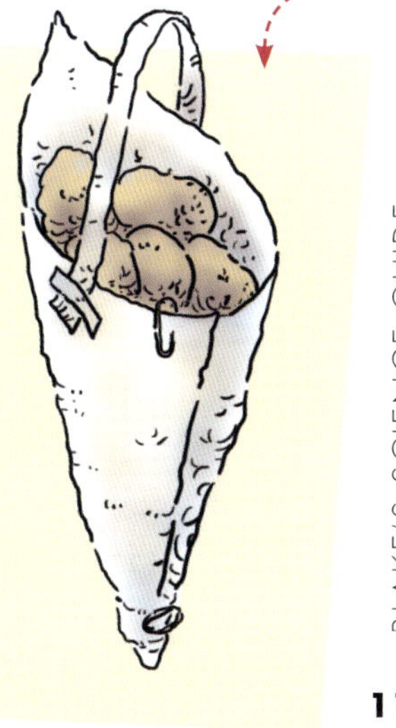

Structures may have to:

- hold up or support something such as a water tank or a book case.
- reach across or span a distance such as a bridge or a roof. A crane reaches across a distance but its load is balanced by a counter weight.
- contain or protect something such as a pet's travel cage or an egg carton.

Example

A soft-drink can must be strong enough to:

- *withstand the gas pressure inside*
- *withstand knocks when it is carried around*
- *carry the weight of other cans when they are stacked on top of one another.*

The can must also have a weak point for easy opening.
An empty can will support you if you stand on top of it but it will collapse if you squeeze its side – it is strong in one way but weak in another.

Try this

Students built the marshmallow sky scraper below, as part of a test.
Before they started, they considered:

- how both of the materials (marshmallow and toothpicks) behave
- how the materials might join together
- how the materials might strengthen each other.

However, they had trouble getting the structure high enough and it eventually fell over.

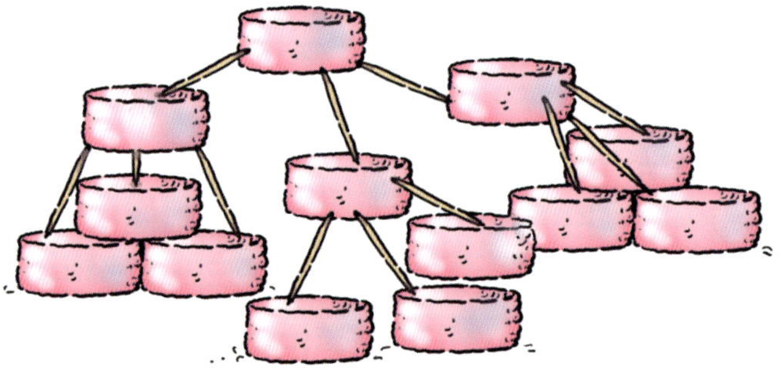

1 Which shapes appear to be the strongest in this structure?
2 What is it about marshmallow that limits its use as a building material?
3 Comment on the joins between the marshmallows and the toothpicks.
4 Would there be any advantage in having more than one toothpick coming out of each marshmallow?

PILES AND PILES OF GARBAGE

There was a time when people used materials over and over again. They would never have thought of using a material only once and then throwing it away. Today, we are surrounded by things that are made to be thrown away.

Millions of kilograms of materials are made by factories using precious fossil fuels and energy. They are used and then thrown away. All this garbage just keeps piling up. More than one third of our garbage is paper; the rest is yard waste, food, metals, glass and plastics.

About one third of what we throw out started as packaging. Some packaging serves a purpose but most is just there to attract attention so that you buy one product instead of another. You may even buy something that you don't even want just because of the way it is packaged.

When you throw something into the garbage, it doesn't just disappear!

Processing garbage

Garbage has to be processed in some way. Most of the garbage is taken to a landfill where it is compacted and buried, but not every material can break down. Landfills are really not such a great idea as cities are running out of places to put them. Some garbage is taken to incinerators and burned. These methods of disposal can cause serious environmental damage.

Example

Sometimes hazardous waste such as batteries, medicines, chemicals, oil and oven cleaners is buried. Hazardous chemicals can leak out of the landfill and damage the surrounding environment.
Not all materials will burn easily. Some produce dangerous gases and the ash that is left over can contain dangerous metals such as lead and cadmium.

Try this

Strong winds can blow plastics around and they can end up in rivers. Some people drop plastic garbage into the ocean and hope it just disappears! If plastic garbage does find its way to the ocean, it will kill sea creatures by the thousands. How does plastic kill sea creatures?

Scientists are working on ways to make packaging more environmentally friendly

Biodegradable materials

Biodegradable materials are easily recycled by the chemical processes of living things like fungi, bacteria, earthworms. These organisms need plenty of air, water and warmth to operate. Paper biodegrades but polystyrene does not.

Once a container is in a landfill, it will not biodegrade if there is not enough water or air. Carrots that had been in a landfill for 20 years were dug up and found to still look just like carrots!

Fast food containers

Recently, attention has been directed at the garbage created by fast food restaurants. These places use enormous amounts of paper and plastics for packaging their food. Unfortunately, these materials are thrown away and end up in landfills. Making decisions about packaging involves looking at the costs and energy involved in producing it as well as disposing of the material later.

Example

With every cheeseburger deal (burger, can of soft drink, fries), comes a side order of garbage. The things we eat are the bun, the cheese, the sauce, the fries and the soft drink. The garbage that we happily pay for as well is the burger container (polystyrene), the drink container (aluminium), the fries bag (paper), the serviettes (paper), the cutlery (plastic) and carry bag (plastic).

Environmental problems are hard to solve because people see things differently.

1. Should fast food outlets make you bring your own plate and cup?
2. What types of waste occurs in restaurants where they supply plates, cups and cutlery?

Try this

Recycling materials

When nature has used a natural resource, it always recycles it. Nature never stops recycling. Rocks, nutrients and water are examples of how nature recycles materials.

Energy is needed to recycle materials, but recycling is better than throwing the materials away. Half the things that people throw away can be recycled. Recycling leads to less rubbish in landfills and more room for things that cannot be recycled. Many communities have recycling programs for paper, glass, cans, plastics and cardboard. Chemical and physical changes can be used to recycle materials.

Example

- *Paper is recycled in factories that shred and mash the paper into pulp, which is then turned back into paper.*
- *Glass is recycled at factories where bottles and jars are broken into tiny bits, melted down and made into new glass.*
- *Aluminium cans are recycled over and over again by being rolled into aluminium sheeting.*
- *Recycled motor oil is as good as new.*

At least 20% of garbage is organic. These nutrients originated in the soil. They can be recycled back into the soil if we compost organic materials. Compost forms when organic matter decays or rots. The decay process is helped by decomposers like bacteria, fungi, earthworms and snails.

Consider the materials in a cheeseburger deal: burger, soft drink, fries, polystyrene burger container, aluminium drink container, the paper fries bag, the paper serviettes, the plastic cutlery and plastic carry bag.

1 Which materials were organic materials?
2 Which materials were biodegradable?
3 Which materials can be recycled?
4 Which materials are destined for land fill?

Recycling plastics

There is growing concern about the environmental impact of plastic garbage. Plastics are difficult to recycle because there are many different types and food is often still attached to the plastic garbage. The plastics industry has developed a uniform coding system. This system identifies containers by material type so they can be sorted for recycling. The code is a three-sided triangular arrow with a number in the centre and letters underneath. The number and the letters indicate the resin (raw chemical) from which the container is made.

Example

One way of separating all the different types of plastics is to use different densities. Water has a density if 1.0, so anything with a density less than one should float and anything with a density greater than 1.0 should sink.

Plastic Type	Letter Code	Uses	Density
Polyethylene	PETE (1)	Carbonated soft drink bottle, clear fruit juice bottles	1.39
High Density Polyethylene	HDPE (2)	Milk bottles, bleach bottle, wheelie bins	0.95–0.94
Polyvinylchloride	V (3)	Transparent shampoo bottles, 'Dettol' bottles, guttering and drainage pipes	1.4
Low density polyethylene	LDPE (4)	Snap lock sandwich bags, cling film, detergent squeeze bottles, garbage bags	0.95–0.97
Polypropylene	PP (5)	Take away food containers, lunch boxes, chip bags	0.90–0.91
Polystyrene	PS (6)	Yoghurt cartons, plastic cutlery	1.0
Expanded polystyrene	EPS (6)	Foam cups, fruit boxes	0.2

This test shown above can be used to sort a mixture of plastics or to find out the name of a plastic that is not known.

1 If an unknown plastic turned up in a recycling station and its density was 1.0, what type of material would it be?

2 What does the term 'density' mean?

Try this

EARTH & SPACE SCIENCES

Earth and space sciences develop knowledge and understanding about the Earth's dynamic structure and its place in the cosmos.

TIME

Time measures the passing of long-term and short-term patterns of events that occur on Earth and in the Universe. Some of these events are days, weeks, months and years.

Atoms are the smallest pieces of a substance

Keeping track of time

Early humans measured the time by the passing of the seasons or by night passing to day. They used tools such as water clocks (water draining from a container), sand clocks (flow of sand at a predictable rate) and sundials (use of shadows relative to the Sun's position). In space, the Moon's orbit of the Earth and the Earth's orbit of the Sun can be used to measure the passage of time.

In the 16th Century, Galileo Galilei discovered a new kind of measurement called – TIME

Example

Modern man uses tools, such as clocks, timers, watches, calendars and alarms, to measure time. Most calendar years are 365 days and one quarter. For convenience, humans invented the leap year, which has 366 days.

Why did humans choose 365 days and one quarter?

Try this

Brain teaser

Humans divide time into the past, the present and the future – the present is continually changing and becoming the past as the future continues to supply us with the present. Think about:

- If there were no humans, would there be a past, a present and a future?
- Do animals and plants operate in the past or in the future or just the present?
- Will time ever end?

Geological time

Geological time is used to track events that have happened on Earth since it was born, 4.6 billion years ago. During this time, the rocks cooled, the oceans and atmosphere formed, weather patterns began, several ice ages came and went, large meteorites crashed into the planet, several mass extinctions happened, mammals took over from the dinosaurs, and man evolved. Also, for all these years the landscape was being sculptured into what we have today. Scientists have worked out a timeline on all of this by using tools such as carbon dating and fossil recording. They have put all the events into a time chart.

The last living thing to have touched a rock may well have been a dinosaur!

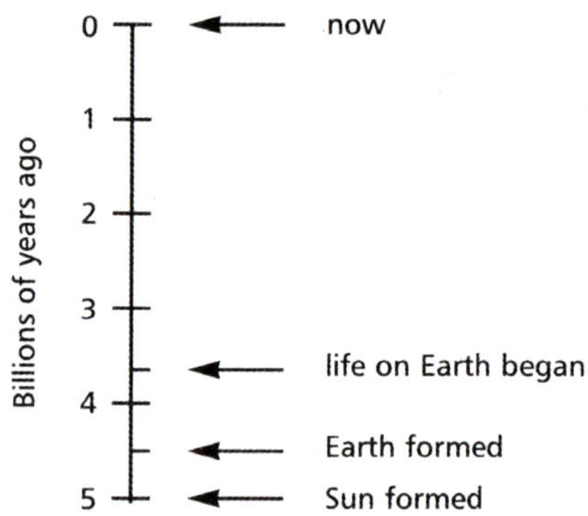

Try this

Example

Look at the time chart. About 3.7 billion years ago life began on Earth.

Dinosaurs became extinct about 65 million years ago. Mark this place on the time chart.

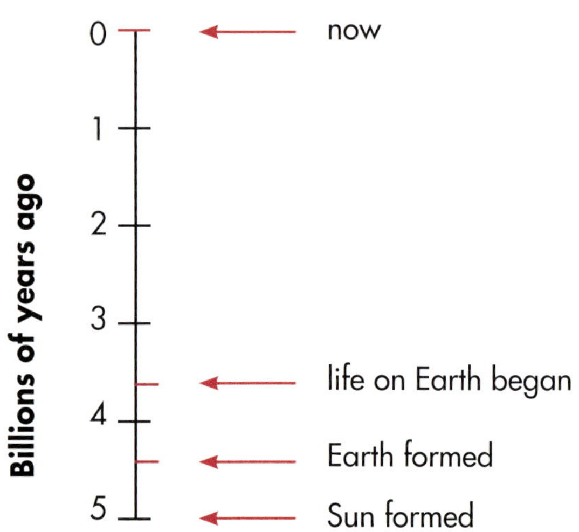

PLANET EARTH

Earth is a tiny, oddly shaped ball among countless billions scattered throughout the universe.

The Earth in space

Our **planet** is part of a system of planets orbiting around a star. It is one of a ring of eight planets circling the Sun, making up our **solar system**.

We see planets because they reflect the light from the Sun. The **Sun** is one of 100 billion stars in our **galaxy**. Our galaxy, the **Milky Way**, is one of 10 billion galaxies scattered throughout the Universe.

You have only to look up into the sky at night to see more stars. Stars give out their own light, unlike the planets. Stars are fixed in space and do not move around like the planets. They stay in the same patterns (constellations); for example, Orion and Centaurus. Our Sun, one way or another, provides us with most of our energy.

Dimensions of time and scale

How big is big!

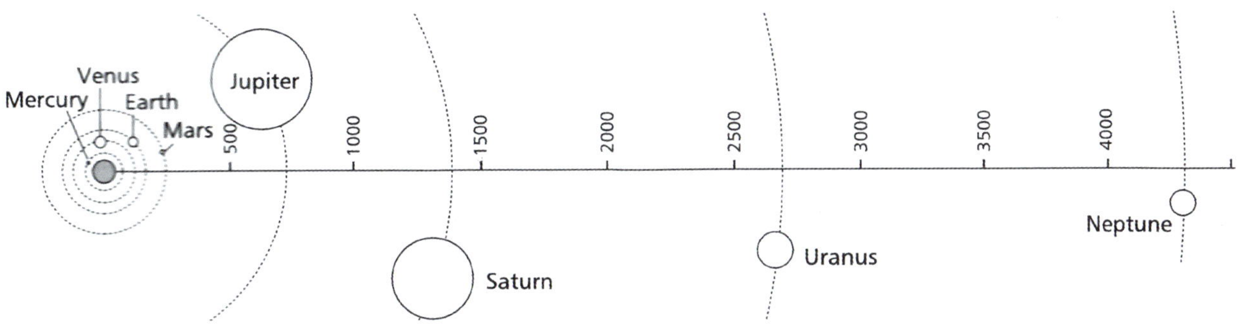

The Universe is made up of distances too vast to reach and particles too small to see, and definitely too numerous to count!

'The total number of stars in the Universe is larger than all the grains of sand of all the beaches of planet Earth.'
Carl Sagan

The distances in space are far too great for the human mind to grasp easily, but we will try!

Example

Look at the diagram on the previous page. By estimating, we can work we can work out that Uranus is about 2 650 million kilometres away from the Sun.

Try this

Study the diagram on the previous page. How far is the biggest planet from the smallest planet?

Distance in space

Distance in space is so large that it is measured using light, because light travels faster than anything else (300 000 kilometres per second). A **light year** is the distance that light travels in one year. Alpha Centauri is our next closest sun but it is in the next solar system and it is 4.3 light years away.

Example

Study the diagram of our galaxy. The Milky Way is shaped like a flying saucer. It is 100 000 light years long and 40 000 light years wide. Our solar system measures about two thirds across the Milky Way's diameter.

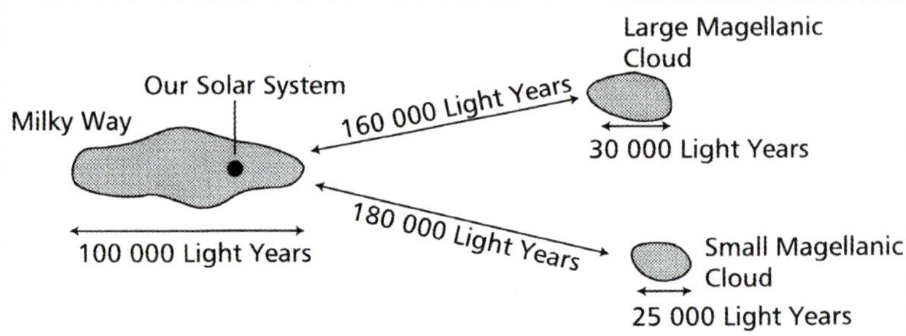

Try this

How far is it from our solar system to our nearest galaxy?

Third rock from the Sun

No-one knows how the Earth came to exist, but one theory is that the Earth formed over billions of years from a whirling cloud of gas and dust. The cloud circled the Sun, which was at the time a new star. The effects of static electricity and gravity could have caused the dust particles to lump together, gradually forming a larger body.

The Earth is 4.6 billion years old.

Forces at work in our solar system

- **Gravity** holds everything together in our solar system. For example, gravity helps the atmosphere stay in place around the Earth, causes the tides on Earth (Moon's gravity) and stabilises the wobbling of our planet as it moves around the Sun. The Moon has less mass than the Earth so its gravity is much weaker. Astronauts weigh one sixth of their normal weight when they are on the Moon.
- **Magnetism** is another invisible force that dictates how the Earth works. The Earth is a magnet bigger than all others, complete with a magnetic north pole and a south pole. The iron core of the Earth, as it spins, acts like a dynamo on a bicycle – generating electricity and turning Earth into a giant magnet. The magnetosphere extends 60 000 kilometres into space and can deflect objects like meteors away from the Earth.

Example
Magnetism helps to protect the Earth from marauding meteors by repelling stray bits of space debris and rocks that may otherwise slam into it.

Which invisible force holds the Universe together?

Try this

Earth's rotations

Changes on Earth, such as day and night and the seasons, relate to the Earth's rotation on its own **axis** and its orbit around the Sun. Our Earth spins at 800 km/h and hurtles through space at 80 000 km/h.

Earth's poles

The Earth's geographical north and south poles fall on the axis (tilted by 23.5 degrees) around which the Earth spins. The magnetic north and south poles are in different positions and are slowly but continually shifting. The magnetic poles actually swap completely every few hundred years.

Earth spins at 800 kilometres per hour

Shadows

Shadows are shortest at midday when the Earth turns to face the Sun directly. Shadows are the longest at sunrise, at sunset and in winter. Night falls when the Earth spins so far around that we face away from the Sun. The term 'am' refers to the 12 hours before the Sun is directly overhead, and 'pm' is the 12 hours after the Sun is directly overhead.

Night and day

Once every 24 hours, the Earth revolves on its geographical axis.
It always spins in the same direction towards the east. So the Sun appears in the east every day, goes right overhead at midday and disappears in the west.
It is this rotation that gives us day and night. Of course, even though the Sun appears to rise and fall, it is the Earth and you that are moving, not the Sun.

What would happen if the Moon stopped moving?

The reason for seasons

It takes one year for the Earth to spin around the Sun. This yearly rotation and the tilted axis of the Earth cause seasonal changes. There are four seasons, summer, autumn, winter and spring. In the southern hemisphere, in summer, the south pole is tilted towards the Sun so we have long summer days. In winter, the south pole is tilted away from the Sun so the winter days are shorter. This is reversed in the northern hemisphere.

Example

If the Earth stopped spinning, the side facing the Sun would stay extremely hot and the other side of the Earth would be extremely cold. Life as we know it could not exist.

The Moon

The Moon is a **satellite** spinning around the Earth. It has been caught by the Earth's gravitational pull. The Moon has no light of its own but reflects the light of the Sun. The Moon takes one month to orbit once around the Earth and the same time to spin on its own axis. This means that the same side of the Moon is always facing the Sun. The Moon is always half in sun and half in shade. This gives us the **phases of the moon**. The Moon does not have an atmosphere so you can see the **craters** left in its surface by lumps of space rock that have crashed into it.

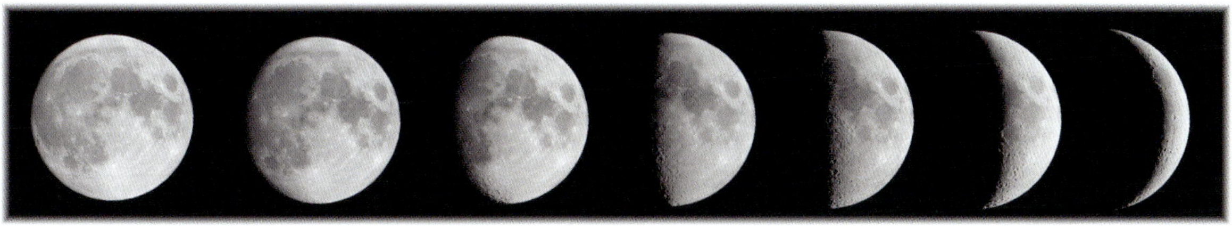

What is an eclipse?

An **eclipse** occurs when one heavenly body obscures another. A solar eclipse occurs when the Moon passes directly between the Earth and the Sun. It hides the Sun from view. In a lunar eclipse, the Moon passes into the Earth's shadow and the Earth blocks the Sun's light from the Moon.

Example

Study the diagram of a solar eclipse and notice that the Moon is hiding the Sun.

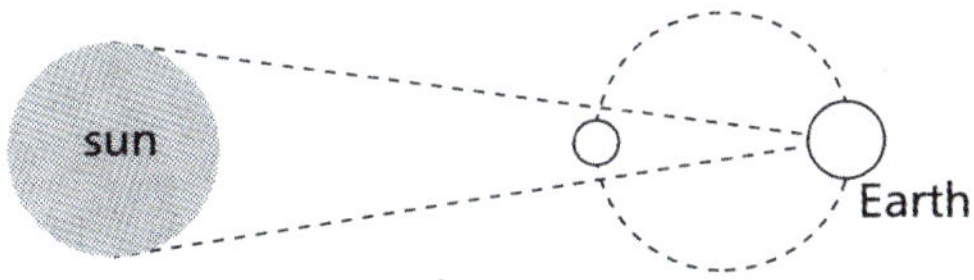

Solar eclipse

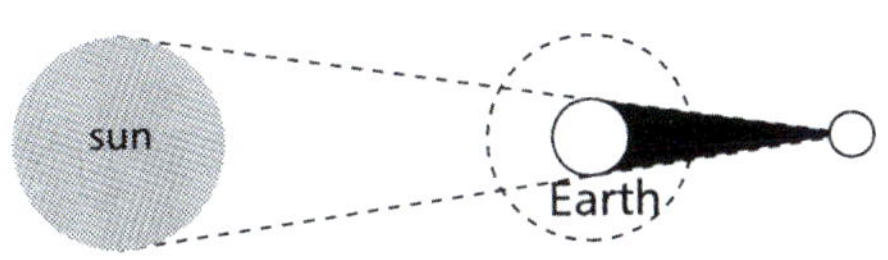

Lunar eclipse

In a lunar eclipse, which body blocks the Sun's light from the Moon?

Try this

Other curious neighbours

We know that we live in a dangerous neighbourhood – just ask the dinosaurs! When the solar system was formed, there were leftovers – chunks of rock, dust and ice that spin around in space and cross the paths of the planets as they move around the Sun.

- **Asteroids** are bits of rock and metal between Mars and Jupiter and are believed to be leftover from the formation of the planets.
- **Comets** are a mass of frozen gases and dust that orbit the Sun. Halley's comet is the most famous.
- A **meteoroid** is a chunk of rock, ice and metal drifting in space. When a meteoroid hits the Earth's atmosphere the friction between the air and the meteoroid causes the air close to it to get hot and glow. It becomes a **meteor** (shooting star) with a fiery tail.
- A **meteorite** is a meteor that is not totally burned up and hits the Earth. It is believed that a very large meteorite hit the American continent and was responsible for the end of the dinosaurs, 65 million years ago. Other amazing things to research are black holes, neutron stars, pulsars, quasars, dark matter and black energy.

Example

We are not alone. We share our space neighbourhood with the eight planets of our solar system, 50 moons, billions of stars, 100 000 asteroids, millions of comets, and millions of tiny fragments of rock and metal and so much more.

Space age

The 'space age' is about 200 years old. Our civilisation has benefited greatly not only from NASA's space program in USA but from those of many other countries. Our civilization is totally dependent on a host of satellites that orbit the Earth. These satellites provide global communications, weather forecasting and information services such as banks and postal services. If anything happened to our space systems it would be chaos on Earth.

Try this

Planet Earth – 149 million kilometres from the Sun, somewhere in the space between Venus and Mars. If you can find our moon, you will find us! What is our space address?

STRUCTURE OF THE EARTH

We know very little about what happens beneath our feet. Since the day it was born, this lump of rock that we call Earth has continued to churn away with enormous forces! This power can cause sudden geological events that can change the Earth's surfaces. The effects of these changes are only evident when viewed over extremely long timescales.

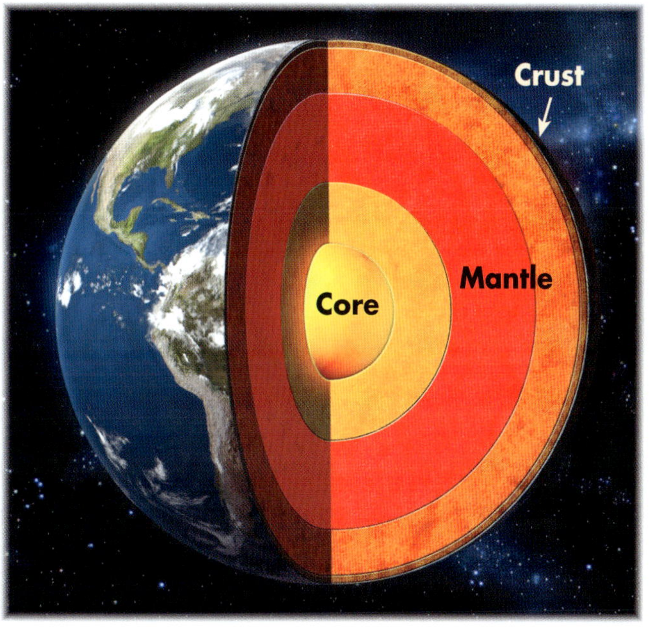

The rock on which you sit today is almost round, like a ball, but its surface has been crumpled and broken. The centre is a fiery furnace, hot enough to melt rock. It is an unbelievably hot and high pressure area made of rock and metals called the **core**.

The next section of the Earth is called the **mantle**. It is a rocky shell that encloses the hot core.

The **crust** of the Earth, which is up to 70 kilometres thick, is the outer layer of the Earth. This is made of several enormous slabs of cooled rock called tectonic plates. These plates are always slowly on the move, around the planet, bumping and banging into each other.
This outermost surface of the planet is where animals and plants can exist.

The crust is a thin, tortured, crumpled, twisted, and brittle skin of rock on the surface of the planet.

Example

Nobody has ever been to the core or to the mantle of the Earth, but lots of us have been inside the crust. If you have been in a cave, a mine or a big hole, you have taken a look around the inside the Earth's crust.

Try this

The Earth's crust is a bit like the cracked shell of an egg. Explain how the Earth's crust is similar to an egg shell.

Example

Look out the window. You can see some of the scars from all this abuse – hills, mountains, rivers, flatlands, cliffs and gorges.

How do scientists view and record the different features on the surface of the Earth? Hint: we use this record to help guide us on our travels.

Try this

Changing landscapes

The Earth's crust has been subjected to billions of years of physical abuse.

- Earth's surface has been scratched, worn, split, buried, raked, drained, stretched, kicked, flattened, flooded and fired.
- Huge mountain ranges have come and also gone.
- Continents of ice have gouged and bulldozed the crust repeatedly.

Earth's soils

Over millions of years, the weathering process has shaped the Earth's crust, by breaking up the rock and producing the soils that we use to grow our food. Over millions of years, weathering and **erosion** of the rock has changed the surface of the Earth and continues to do so.

Weathering mechanisms

- Heating rocks causes them to expand. Cooling rocks causes them to contract. Constant heating and cooling can make rocks crack.
- Rainwater expands when it freezes, and if it gets into the cracks in rocks it can crack the rock further, or even break pieces off when it expands.
- Bits of dust and sand blown by the wind can wear away the rocks like sandpaper.
- If seeds germinate in the cracks of rocks their roots force the cracks open further.
- Acid gases in the air also attack rocks. Carbon dioxide dissolves in water to make a weak acid that reacts with some rocks like limestone, chalk and marble. Over thousands of years, this reaction can dissolve the rocks away.
- Chemicals dissolved in water can react with minerals in the rocks to produce completely new substances. This causes the rock to become weaker, easier to split and it will crumble into smaller bits.

Example

Sandblasting of exposed cliffs continually changes the coastline, and the extremely hot days and very cold nights of central Australia cause the rocks to break up.
The sandstone structures in Europe and the Sphinx in Egypt are victims of **acid rain**.

Complete the flow chart below by adding the following types of weathering to the boxes.

Physical (wind, water, ice)
Chemical (acid rain, rusting)
Biological (plants, animals)

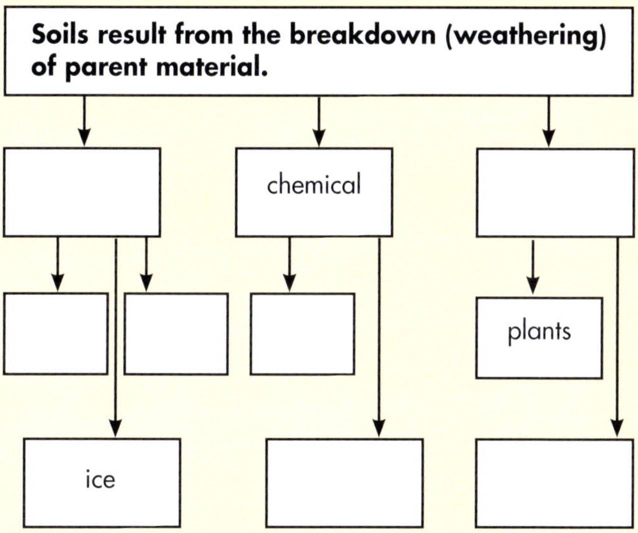

What is the difference between a rock and a mineral?

Rocks are not minerals. Rocks are made of a collection, or a 'mixture', of many minerals. A mineral is a chemical compound (a combination of elements) found naturally in the rocks of the Earth. For example, iron ore, a ruby, gold and quartz are minerals. We know of about 2000 different minerals but only 12 of them are common to most rocks. When rain falls on rocks, it dissolves some of the minerals out of the rocks and helps in the weathering process.

A recipe for soil

When you look at the ground around you, the most common thing you see is soil. The soil is only a thin 'blanket' covering the bedrock (igneous rock). It takes thousands of years for the Earth to make soil. We grow our food in the soil. If we do not look after the soil (if it blows away or washes away) we will lose it and we cannot wait around for a few thousand years to get some more!

To create soil:

Step 1 – Break big rocks into small rocks, then into rock fragments, then into rock grains and rock dust.

Step 2 – Mix these rock grains and dust with air, water, organic material (dead and alive plants, animals and dung), some recycling organisms (fungi, moulds and earthworms) and you have very rich SOIL!

Soil on the move

Once the rocks have been weathered into rock grains or soil, natural forces move them about. This process is called erosion. Over millions of years, soil movement has changed the shape of the Earth. Erosion levels mountains and helps build up **sedimentary rocks**.

Soil moves by:

- windstorms swirling away huge amounts of dry soil
- glaciers scraping rocks along the ground like giant sandpaper, for long distances
- running water causing creek banks to erode away, gullies to form and hillsides to slip.

Rebuilding the crust

The Earth is constantly recycling itself. There are no original rocks left on the planet they have all been ground to dust, melted and been reborn time after time. Just as the crust is constantly broken down, it is constantly rebuilt.

The old and battered rocks of the crust are continually forced back into the mantle where the plates meet. This process is called **subduction**.

The rocks are churned around and mixed in with the rich, new, hot rock in the mantle and then regularly ejected back out onto the surface of the planet again through volcanoes. The crust is constantly renewed and rebuilt by this process termed the rock cycle.

Example

Countries such as New Guinea, New Zealand and parts of Asia have incredibly rich soils because volcanoes are regularly renewing the rock on the surface. In Australia, we have no active volcanoes so our soils are old, weathered and nutrient poor.

Explain what is going on in the diagram.

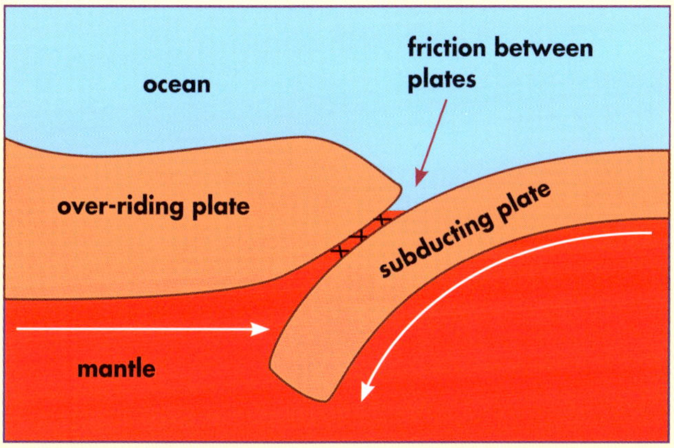

Try this

Geo-superstars

Not far beneath your feet the pressures and temperatures are immense, causing the inside of the Earth to toss about with unimaginable forces. This tumultuous power can make the ground shake, throw up mountain ranges, release the awesome spectacle of volcanoes and force continents to crash together or to rip apart. The edges of the tectonic plates are the sites of this intense geological activity and are responsible for changing the face of the Earth. The plates are always moving, sliding over and under each other and even colliding with each other. They move slowly over small distances of around 2.5 – 5.0 centimetres a year.

Volcanoes

Volcanoes occur at plate boundaries. A volcano is an opening, like a safety valve, in the Earth's crust.

Through the opening **magma**, gases, solid rock fragments, poisonous fumes and ash can be discharged. Lava flows from the top of the volcano down the sides. This is brand new, mineral-rich rock and once weathered, forms soil that will grow practically anything.

There are about 1000 active or potentially active volcanoes in the world. The greatest activity in our part of the world is in the 'Ring of Fire' around the Pacific Ocean. Australia has very few volcanoes or earthquakes because we are in the middle of a plate and do not have plate boundaries crossing the country.

How do volcanoes form?

In the Earth's mantle, underneath a volcano, there are pockets of a hot, liquid-like mixture of rocks and gases. When heat and pressure build up and the gases expand, an eruption occurs.

The magma is forced up the pipe and flows out as lava onto the surface of the Earth. This relieves the pressure in the volcano. As this lava cools, it forms new rocks that are rich in minerals.

Big volcanoes can produce a staggering amount of ash and colossal amounts of gas such as sulphur dioxide. The ash and the gas can cause catastrophic damage to plants and animals and alter the landscape and the climate.

Example *This article was released after a volcanic eruption changed the landscape on an island in the Pacific Ocean in 2009.*

Media Release – December 2009

Volcano Blasts Island

A volcanic eruption with a magnitude of 7.9 occurred on the small pacific islet of Hunga Ha'apia, close to Tonga. It destroyed rich birdlife, fish and vegetation, leaving a wasteland of black ash and tree stumps. Tonga lies on the 'Pacific Ring of Fire' where continental plates collide causing regular volcanic and seismic activity.

Media Release – 18 May 1980

'Mt St Helens Blows Out'

When the north side of Mt St Helens (Washington State), bulged and then popped like an enormous bubble, it was with a force equal to 500 atomic bombs. Fuelled by super-heated gas, the eruption stripped 500 metres off the summit and one billion cubic metres of pulverized rock, ice and mud flowed more than 30 km consuming everything in its path.

Read the information in the media release above. How did this eruption change the landscape?

Try this

Earthquakes

When tectonic plates collide head-on or sideswipe each other, they can sometimes get locked together. When they jolt free, a tremendous amount of energy is involved. Most of these jolts are not serious, but every now and then a particularly big jolt occurs and causes landslides, avalanches, mudslides, tsunamis and the demolition of man-made structures. Small jolts are called tremors and big jolts are called **earthquakes**.

Building mountains

Plates can push against each other, compressing and folding the land upwards into mountains over millions of years. The Earth can also crack under pressure. This is called faulting. The Andes and the Himalayan Mountains are still being formed as one plate pushes up against another causing crumpling, earthquakes and volcanoes.

Example

Refer back to the diagram of the subduction process. When a subducting plate gets jammed on the overriding plate and then ruptures, part of the crust moves and we experience an earthquake.

If these two plates were pushing against each other instead of one going under the other, what would be happening to the Earth's landscape?

Tsunamis

Tsunamis are gigantic, destructive waves mostly caused by an underwater earthquake resulting in a sudden rise or fall of a section of the Earth's crust. They can also be caused by underwater landslides, volcanic eruptions, land slumping into the ocean or meteorite impacts. Tsunami waves are so powerful because, unlike normal ocean waves, they involve water movement right to the sea floor.

A tsunami races along at hundreds of kilometres an hour with wave crests more than a 100 kilometres apart. As it approaches shallower water, it slows down and gets higher. Finally, the wall of water slams into the coast.

The tsunami in Sumatra resulted from the Andaman Island earthquake. This was the fourth largest earthquake in the world with a magnitude of 9.0 on the Richter scale. It happened at the interface of the India and Burma plates, where the Burma plate subducted below the India plate. Millions of people were displaced from their homes or died.

Examples of major Tsunami events are:
1933 – Honshu, Japan (over 3000 deaths)
1960 – Hilo Harbour, Hawaii (23 million dollars damage, 61 deaths)
2004 – Sumatra
2011 – Japan

Cross-section of the coast during a Tsunami

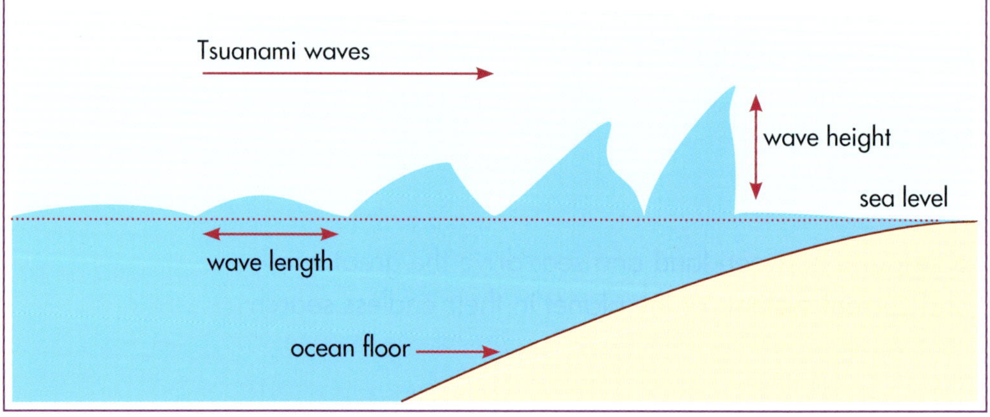

Tsunami warnings

Australia has set up its own warning system – the Australian Tsunami Warning System (ATWS).
The Pacific Tsunami Warning Centre (PTWC) in Hawaii and the Japan Meteorological Agency (JMA) also provide advice for the Pacific and Indian Oceans.

WEATHER

We live between the rocky shell of the Earth and the restless ocean of air called the atmosphere.

What is the atmosphere?

The atmosphere is a thin layer of gases wrapped around the Earth and held in place by the Earth's gravity. This layer provides the air we breathe and the water we drink.

Atmospheric water vapour and carbon dioxide produce the **greenhouse effect**, which keeps temperatures at the surface in the range suitable for life. The layer of **ozone** protects living things from the Sun's deadly ultraviolet light.

The atmosphere is full of microscopic particles like dust, soot, pollen and salt from the oceans. Humans also add chemical particles from car exhaust and factories. The atmosphere is continually adjusting and repairing itself. It is the atmosphere that is responsible for the wide range of climatic regimes over the Earth, providing a diverse array of environments where species have been able to evolve.

When the Atmosphere is on the move we have changing weather patterns

Atmosphere and weather

All atmospheric movement, from coastal sea breezes to monsoons and cyclones is powered by the Sun's energy. It stirs the atmosphere into motion, creating **weather** conditions such as wind, rain, clouds and snow. The Sun's energy is distributed unevenly around the world, which sets up currents in the atmosphere and the oceans. The temperature differences between the equator and the poles, and between land and sea, drive the great wind and current systems of the planet in their endless search for thermal equilibrium. This process, whereby hot and cold molecules move around in the atmosphere and the oceans, is called **convection**.

The Sun also warms the Earth's surface. As the Earth heats up, it radiates heat into the atmosphere, the air particles heat up and atmospheric pressure increases. The Earth's constantly changing weather is a combination of air pressure, air temperature, relative humidity, wind speed and direction, cloud cover and precipitation.

Wind

Wind is created by air molecules moving. Air always moves from an area of high pressure to an area of low pressure in a constant battle trying to equalise pressure everywhere. Sometimes air moves fast (strong winds) sometimes it moves slow (gentle breeze). The energy involved in extreme air movement such as hurricanes, cyclones, twisters and gale force winds can cause enormous amounts of damage to both the natural and built environments.

Example

Contracting and expanding air molecules in the atmosphere result in sea and land breezes. During the day, warm air over the land expands and rises (pressure lowers). Cool sea breezes then force their way underneath. At night, the air cools and contracts over land (high pressure). These cooler breezes from the land then flow back out to sea.

What do we call the air molecules in the atmosphere that are moving from one place on Earth to another?

How wind blows

The Coriolis Effect of the Earth is the force that causes moving objects on the surface of the Earth to appear to veer to the right in the northern hemisphere and to the left in the southern. Winds do not blow in a straight line from high to low pressure zones. They are deflected by the effect of the Earth's rotation. In the northern hemisphere, deflection is to the right and in the southern hemisphere it is to the left. This force affects ocean currents, controls the rotation of hurricanes and typhoons, and affects the flights of aircraft.

Try this

In which direction do the winds spin in the tropical lows termed cyclones that form in Australia?

Example

Hurricanes are low pressure systems that form in the Northern Hemisphere and spin anti-clockwise.

Water and weather

Without water vapour there would be no major weather systems and no life on Earth.

Water on the move is responsible for weather such as humidity, rain, snow, fog and hail.

Water cycle

Water cannot be added to, or subtracted from, the planet. The volume of water on Earth never changes. The rate that water moves through the oceans, rivers and land does change. For example, a water molecule may remain caught in ice for 10 000 years before it moves on. Water is in constant motion. The Earth's water circulation system is referred to as the 'Water Cycle.'

When energy is added to water (in rivers, lakes, oceans, dams), it changes into water vapour (**evaporation**). Water vapour in the air causes humidity. When water vapour in the air moves from the surface of the planet into the colder areas high above, it is cooled (energy is removed). The water vapour **condenses** onto dust particles in the atmosphere, forming clouds. When the droplets of water get bigger and weigh more, gravity pulls the raindrops down from the clouds to Earth (precipitation).

Example

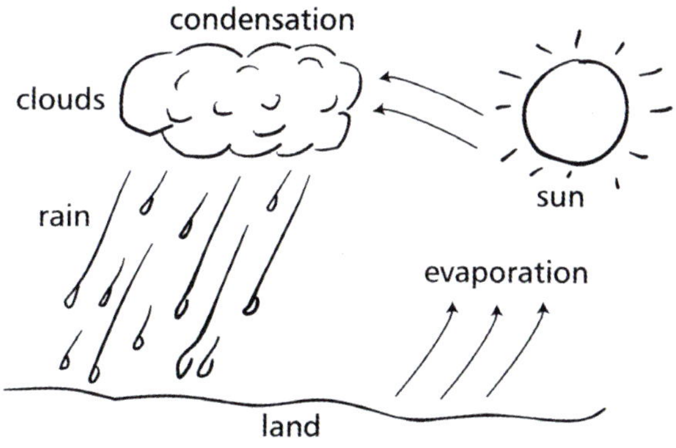

The Water Cycle

The Earth's crust is always at the mercy of the weather

1 Clouds form so that the evaporated water can return to Earth as precipitation. If we consider all the rain that falls, then why don't the oceans overflow?

2 Can we make more water if the water on Earth runs out?

Try this

The water cycle is the biggest desalination plant on Earth

Oceans and weather

The real force that determines the weather is the oceans. Meteorologists tend to treat the oceans and the atmosphere as a single system. Seawater is nearly always on the move as waves and currents. The ocean's currents transfer the Sun's heat and help to create the Earth's climates.

Currents

The Coriolis Effect influences the oceans. Currents in the northern hemisphere rotate clockwise and those in the southern hemisphere rotate anticlockwise. Water temperature differences and salinity also impact on the currents.

Waves

It takes very little wind to make a wave. However, the bigger the wind, the bigger the waves, and the more energy they have to inflict on coastlines. Waves never stop pounding against the shores of continents and islands. The energy of a wave breaks down the coastline into rubble. These waves then carry the rubble to another place where the coastline is re-built. The shape of Earth's coastal areas is forever changing.

Climate and weather

Climate refers to the average weather conditions of a particular place. These weather conditions are measured and recorded every day. The climate of an area is vital to life and helps to shape ecosystems. Scientists are still struggling to explain how the Sun's energy is moved around the Earth by the atmosphere and oceans to create our climate. They are also battling with understanding immediate problems like **global warming**, ozone depletion, and with predicting tsunamis and volcanic eruptions.

Australia's climate

Europe has a harsh but predictable climate year after year, and is therefore capable of maintaining an enormous biomass. No matter how harsh the climate is, food can be grown and stored. However, Australia is the only continent on Earth where the most overwhelming influence on climate is an irregular, non-annual climatic change. The cycle driving Australia's unpredictable climate is called the **El Nino Southern Oscillation** (ENSO).

What is ENSO?

ENSO is the flow of warm surface water back and forth across the Pacific Ocean. The weather patterns are opposite on both sides of the Pacific Ocean, depending on the position of the warm water. The warm water is normally kept around Indonesia, New Guinea and Northern Australia by the prevailing winds (La Nina). Evaporation is high, clouds form and good rainfall persists. If the winds weaken, an El Nino event begins in Australia and the warm water flows back east to the coastline of Peru and Equador.

It is only in Australia that a whole continent is held in the grip of the ENSO

ENSO in South America

In South America, the warm water floats on top of the cold water and does not mix. This causes the weather to change and the coast is lashed by terrible storms that batter the land, washing millions of tonnes of soil down off the mountains, destroying towns and cities.

ENSO in Australia

However, in Australia, the sea is colder, no clouds form, rainfall decreases and droughts persist. Eventually, the west pacific winds re-establish themselves and the warm water moves back across the Pacific Ocean and accumulates along the Australian coast. Water evaporates, clouds form and the drought breaks, often with floods and severe storms. This La Nina situation develops along the north Australian coastline. Peru returns to a drought situation.

Southern Oscillation

The movement of this warm water, back and forth, across the Pacific Ocean, termed the Southern Oscillation, is now measured by recording sea surface temperatures using buoys across the ocean. The Southern Oscillation Index (SOI) is a measure of the strength and phase of the Southern Oscillation. Negative values in the Southern Oscillation indicate an El Nino event resulting in drought in Australia and positive values indicate a La Nina event (rain).

Example

During 2009–10 a La Nina situation developed along the north Australian coast and the drought was broken. During January 2011, record breaking rain fell resulting in devastating floods throughout Queensland. The Southern Oscillation index for this event was 'positive 8' – indicating a stronger than normal La Nina situation. The warm water also encouraged a more severe cyclone season. Tropical Cyclone Yasi (January 2011) was the biggest system ever recorded on the Queensland Coast.

Study the following graph of the progress of a typical El Nino event over 18 months.

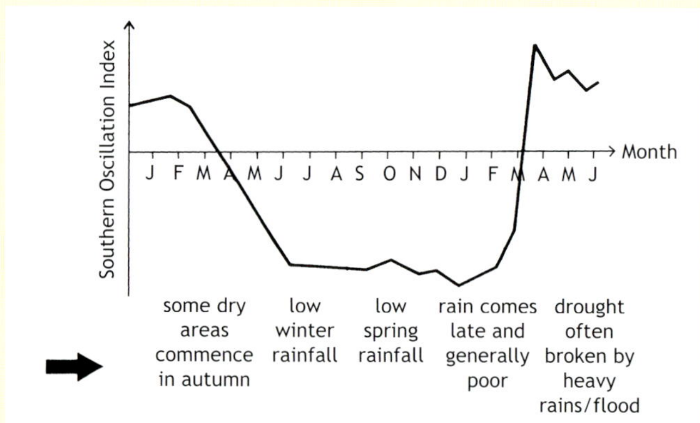

1 In which month does a negative SOI begin?

2 How many months experience a positive El Nino event?

3 What weather features occur in the negative SOI period?

Try this

How long does ENSO last?

The length of ENSO is extremely variable and scientists do not really know how long it has been operating – it could be a couple of hundred or maybe millions of years old. However, it is a very significant part of Australia's climate and yet it remained undiscovered for so long.

EARTH'S RESOURCES AND HUMAN ACTIVITY

The more planets that astronomers discover, the more exceptional the Earth appears. Earth seems to have just the right combination of size, distance from the Sun, spin rate and atmospheric ingredients for it to be home to all the creatures great and small that call Earth 'Home'.

We live on top of the Earth`s crust, but this is only part of our environment. The Earth`s atmosphere, water and soil are the foundations of our environment. How we live and what we do affects these resources as everything is connected. We are beginning to realise that human-based developments, such as acid rain, polluted air and water, and accidental erosion of soils, is damaging the environment and the way we live.

Humans are the keepers of the Earth

Atmosphere and life

Life and the atmosphere have had a long and complex relationship. The atmosphere is quite different now compared to when the Earth was first formed. There were large amounts of carbon dioxide and practically no oxygen. What caused the massive reversal was the development of life – the impact of life on the atmosphere was profound! Recently, scientists have been suggesting that life and the atmosphere may no longer be in balance.

Some of the most extensive, but least visible, human impact has been on the atmosphere. Scientists believe that human activity is causing a depletion of the ozone layer as well as an enhancement of the greenhouse effect. Most scientists agree that these things are happening but there is still much discussion about what may be causing these changes in the atmosphere and also what the long term consequences for life on the planet may be.

Example

As the Earth aged, the atmosphere changed. Carbon dioxide was dissolved into the oceans, fixed into the structure of plants and set in carbonate sediments like limestone. Large amounts of oxygen began to be produced and released into the atmosphere by plants as they evolved.

Try this

List the resources that are the absolute foundations of life.

It is not the quantity of air that we need but rather the quality of it

Global warming

Global warming is a term used to explain a gradual warming of the Earth due to natural and man-made changes. The Earth's atmosphere stops some of the heat that radiates off the Earth from escaping back into space. This heat keeps the planet warm enough for life to exist. Scientists believe that over the last 150 years (since the Industrial Revolution) the burning of fossil fuels has raised the level of carbon dioxide in the atmosphere and therefore the temperature of the Earth.

Compounding this has been the removal of millions of trees that could have helped to absorb the carbon dioxide. Scientists believe that an increasing global temperature may cause major changes in weather patterns and in sea levels.

Ozone

Ozone depletion allows more UV radiation to reach the Earth. This is dangerous for many living things as UV can damage genes, cause cell malfunction and lead to cancer.

Acid rain

Acid rain is where pollutant gases such as carbon dioxide, sulphur dioxide and nitrogen dioxide from burning fossil fuels, from factories and power stations are dissolved in the rain, forming acids. This acidic rain can kill forests, dissolve rock and destroy buildings.

How are modern humans affecting the balance in the atmosphere?

Try this

Example

The evolution of plant life on Earth significantly changed the Earth's atmosphere. There was no oxygen on the planet before plants. Oxygen is poisonous to plants so they excrete it as a waste product – the atmosphere is now 20% oxygen.

Water and life

Water is nearly always on the move, relentlessly recycling itself. Water in its three states (solid, liquid, gas), is the life blood of the planet. It is the most common substance we have and yet, in some parts of the world it is a scarce resource. Three quarters of the Earth is covered by seas and oceans. Oceans are used by many countries, but generally the responsibility of no one country.

Plants also contribute to this water cycling process as they pump water out of the soil, through the plant and out through its leaves as water vapour in a process that is called transpiration. Where there are large forests there is usually more rain.

Water is one of the substances that are essential to life on Earth, after all, water was one factor that resulted in the evolution of life as we know it. The properties of water and how it behaves make it a very special and remarkable substance.

Water and modern humans

Water is the Earth's circulation system. Human activity is causing changes to the rivers and streams that make up this system.

- **Silting** occurs when trees and other vegetation are removed, as water flows very quickly over that land and carries the unprotected soil with it. This soil silts up creeks, river systems and seagrass beds in the oceans.
- **Salinity** happens when salt from the land is washed into rivers and creeks. The increased level of salt kills many aquatic species and reduces aquatic **biodiversity**.
- **Eutrophication** is the process by which all the oxygen in water is used up. Many of the waste substances produced by human activities contain nitrates and phosphates. When these are washed into water they act like fertiliser, and can cause algal blooms. The overgrowth of algae uses up the oxygen in the water, killing other forms of life through oxygen deprivation.

Example

Cities, with their houses, roads, shopping centres and pavements, reduce the amount of rainwater that soaks into the planet's ground water supply, increase the temperature and volume of water runoff, and raise local daily air temperatures.

What effect does tree clearing have on the cycling of water?

Try this

- **Marine pollution** enters the sea via water runoff, sewage, oil spills from tankers and garbage dumping and consists of excess nutrients, synthetic chemicals, plastic, oil, heavy metals and radioactive waste.
- **Habitat destruction** in coastal areas such as mangroves and sea grass are destroyed by expanding areas of human habitation.

Example

Modern humans are compromising the quality of Earth's circulation system by polluting oceans and waterways with silt, salt, rubbish and chemicals through the removal of habitat and the establishment of built environments.

A newspaper article reports that there has been an enormous fish kill in a dam near a major city. Explain how human impact on water probably caused this.

Try this

Soils and life

It is easy to forget that the Earth is made of rock and that the soil is just a thin layer covering the bedrock. It is so thin in some places that the bedrock sticks through it as outcrops. Good fertile soil contains a rich mix of organic matter and the right balance of air, nutrients, water to support plant growth. Only 8% of the Earth's surface is covered with topsoil good enough to grow crops.

Soil and modern humans

Agriculture is the main human agent of change to the Earth's surface.

- **Deforestation** is where the land is completely cleared of vegetation to make space for farming. This deforestation often causes desertification, a process that results in the mineral nutrients in the soil being washed away, turning the fertile land into semi-desert. Loss of forest causes a decrease in biodiversity, contributes to changes in the world's climate and increases levels of greenhouse gases.
- **Soil erosion** occurs when the land is cleared of vegetation and the bare soil is left exposed to wind and water. Overgrazing and constant ploughing compounds the problem by destroying the soil structure. When the soil is washed or blown away, not only is the soil lost, but so are its nutrients. This man-made erosion is the most devastating form of land degradation.

Soil is much more than just little rocks

Salinity occurs when salt accumulates in root zones and on the surface in low-lying areas. Clearing deep-rooted trees can result in the water table rising, bringing dissolved salts to the surface. Irrigation makes the situation worse. Salting of the soil causes severe loss of productive land, soil erosion and loss of native habitats.

Example

In some tropical areas, growing maize is critical for local food supplies. However the process tends to destroy the soil. The natural forest must be clear felled and burnt. Then the constant cultivation of maize over many years causes depletion of soil nutrients until the harvest fails completely. The bare soil then becomes exposed and baked by the sun and the tropical rain washes it away.

Try this

The four stages of human development are listed below. Put them in the correct order and match the comment about man's position in the environment at the time.

A Agriculturalist	**1** Great control over the environment but with many undesirable consequences
B Hunter gatherer	**2** Controlled by the environment
C Industrialist	**3** Man has increased control over the environment
D Primitive man	**4** Man starts to control the environment

HUMAN ENDEAVOUR

Human endeavour develops knowledge and understanding about the unique nature of science.

Science seeks to understand and explain the natural world

WHAT IS SCIENCE?

Science is one way of seeking to understand and explain the natural world. Science provides a reliable base for making decisions, generalising and making predictions. Science is dynamic and scientists are creative.
The scientific process is collaborative. Science matters to everyone. Science is what scientists use to answer the questions.

Limits of science

Science can never deal in exact solutions, so a complete proof of something happening is rarely possible. However, scientists can deal in probabilities. For example, scientists can say that the likelihood of something happening is so small that we can assume it never happens.
Science is not a bunch of facts, it is knowledge that can be challenged, revised, extended and altered as new information arises. A scientist's opinion can change based on the new evidence that is presented.

Example

The scientific journal, Nature, has recently reported that there may be three times more stars in the Universe than previously estimated. The estimate of the number of stars in the Universe is now – 300 sextillion (that is 3 with 23 zeroes after it 300 000 000 000 000 000 000 000).

A long time ago people thought that the Earth was flat and ships would sail off the edge. Do we still think that this is true? Why?

Try this

Research

Research is the process through which new knowledge is discovered. The word research means to 'investigate thoroughly'. Research is something that humans do and there are different forms of research – pure research and applied research.

Example

Pure research *is exploratory research. It is often started by the researcher's curiosity, interest or even a hunch. The results may have no immediate commercial application but may be used for some other idea later.*

Applied research *usually has some practical application in mind, such as which material to use as soles on sports shoes. Pure research happens first then the research is applied to a practical idea.*

The following are pieces of research information for the design of a sports shoe. For each piece of research information, decide whether the research is pure or applied.

1. Understanding the structure of the human foot
2. Finding materials which cushion the foot and minimise shock to the leg
3. Perfecting a shoe design that allows air and smelly odours out
4. Developing an elastomer that is a type of plastic material that can regain its shape after shock

SCIENTIFIC VIEW

The key aspects of a scientific view of the world that bridges our knowledge and understanding across the disciplines of science are:

- patterns
- order and organisation
- form and function
- stability and change
- scale and measurement.

Key aspects

Patterns

Scientists have the ability to observe, recognise and describe patterns of similarity and difference. Scale plays an important role in the observation of patterns such as the pattern of day and night, and microscopic and atomic structures.

Order and organisation

Scientists use knowledge about patterns to organise events and objects into groups. They have criteria to develop and to use classification systems.

Example

Most scientists agree with Cell Theory that states 'all organisms are composed of one or more cells, and those cells have arisen from pre-existing cells'. In other words, there is a chain-of-existence extending from your cells back to the earliest cells, over 3.5 billion years ago.

For a theory to become a law, it must be tested and must apply to all situations that relate to the law. There must be no doubt that it is true.

Form and function

The form or features of living things, or materials, and their functions are based on observable behaviours and physical properties.

Stability and change

Some things appear to remain stable or constant over time and some things are always changing. Some things appear to be stable in one time scale (small or large) but changing in another. Stability may be the result of competing forces working together to maintain balance. Change can be measured by looking for patterns of change through graphs, tables and data analysis.

Scale and measurement

Measuring time (rate of change) and size (spatial scale) enables the comparison of observations.

- Large scale – enormous distances in space
- Small scale – atoms and cells
- Slow process – geological time scale
- Fast process – the passing of one hour in the day

Scientists use relative language such as faster or slower, larger or smaller.

Levels of scientific thought

Hypothesis

A hypothesis is an untested idea. It is the most common level of scientific thought and has the lowest level of certainty.

Theory

A theory is a hypothesis that has been repeatedly tested with little modification such as Theory of Evolution, Plate Tectonic theory and the Big Bang theory.

Law

A law is one of the fundamental underlying principles of how the Universe is organised such as The Laws of Thermodynamics, The Laws of Conservation of Matter and Energy, and Newton's Law of Gravity.

Note: The term 'theory,' when used by the general community for unscientific purposes, is just an untested idea.

Try this

1 What do we call a 'law' before it has been adequately tested?

2 Is 'Murphy's Law' (what can go wrong, will go wrong) a real scientific law?

Scientific literacy

Being scientifically literate means you are able to take control of how you want the world to develop because you have a 'grip' on science. Scientifically literate individuals have the ability to make informed and intelligent decisions. They are able to keep up to date with developments in science.

Scientists are good with words. They can:

- produce a report using the third person
- explain phenomenon such as the water cycle
- use names for abstract concepts such as desalination and condensation
- provide instructions such as ' heat the test tube'
- use common words which have a specific science meaning.

Example

Should we build nuclear power stations in Australia?
Should we allow stem cell research?
These current issues require an opinion that has been carefully thought through.

Try this

A scientifically literate person knows how science works and can identify the difference between fact and opinion. After reading the following headline in a newspaper, a scientifically literate person should ask which of the following questions?

Headline – 'Scientists link mobile phone use to brain tumours'.

A How many people were in the trial?

B Was there a control?

C Was the colour of the phone considered?

D Was there any hypothesis being tested?

E Was there a replication of the study?

F Were both the left and right ears tested?

Scientific numeracy

Scientists have the capacity to recognise and understand the role of maths in the natural world. Scientists can:

- measure things and collect data
- represent and interpret the data from investigations
- use informal units and formal units
- consider reliability in measurement
- produce graphical information
- analyse data
- identify trends and patterns.

Scientific numeracy is based on the metric system.

Example

Time is measured in seconds (s)
Sound is measured in decibels (dB)
Mass is measured in kilograms (kg) or grams (g)
Force is measured in newtons (N)
Length is measured in metres (m)
Energy is measured in joules (J)
Radiation is measured in counts/minute

Try this

Here are other quantities used in science and their corresponding units. Place the correct unit of measurement in the spaces provided.

1 The loudness of the stereo is measured in ________________.

2 Pushes and pulls (forces) are measured in ________________.

3 The radiation levels in a nuclear plant are measured in ________________ using a Geiger counter.

4 How long it takes to run 100 metres is measured in ________________.

SCIENCE INVOLVES PROBLEM SOLVING

Scientists spend a lot of time solving problems. When you try to solve a problem, you try to remember things that you know or can do that might help you. You look for new information about the question. You may also ask yourself what you know about the situation, what more you need to know and what assumptions you are making.

We learn nothing unless we proceed from the known to the unknown

Science tips for solving problems

- See it differently – there is more than one way of doing things.
- Guess what will happen if you do a certain thing.
- Jump in and start trying things.
- Understand the way things work.
- Try a number of strategies.
- Recognise limitations and assess risks.
- Use team work.
- Use your ability to estimate and make decisions.

Example

Irving Langmuir improved the electric light bulb by approaching the problem from the opposite direction. He thought about strategies that you would use and then reversed them.

The problem was that residual air inside the bulb kept causing the filament to burn. Instead of trying to remove the troublesome traces of gas from inside the bulb he pumped a gas into the bulb – an inert gas that would not support combustion.

Try this

Using the example above:

1 What was Langmuir's problem?

2 How did Langmuir apply reverse thinking in order to solve this problem?

3 What group of gases must he have used?

WHAT DO SCIENTISTS DO?

Scientists evaluate claims, investigate ideas, solve problems, draw valid conclusions and develop evidence-based arguments. Scientists need observation skills, imagination and determination.

Example
The following question is an open question because it has several possible answers.
What makes eyes respond to light?

Observation

Observation generates questions. It is important in science to ask questions that can be answered by doing an experiment. A good question can be stated as an idea that can be tested. A **closed question** has only one possible answer and it may be a 'yes' or a 'no'. An **open question** has several possible answers.

A good scientific question must be worth solving and be able to be solved by an investigation.

1 Which question can be solved by an investigation?
- **A** Which one of two brands of chocolate taste the smoothest?
- **B** What is the origin of the Universe?

2 Which question is worth solving?
- **A** How many sand grains are on a beach?
- **B** Why is Australia's Megafauna now extinct?

Visualise

Scientists can do mind experiments. They can visualise meanings, ideas and problems, rather than making scientific discoveries by carrying out practical experiments.

Try this

Example
Einstein worked out all of his theories about time and space in his head.

Isaac Newton's ideas on gravity were inspired by a rather famous incident. Do you know what the incident was that started him thinking?

Field research

Most experiments are carried out in a laboratory although some need to be conducted outside 'in the field'. The advantage of field experiments is that they are observed in a natural setting rather than in a planned laboratory environment. However, in field experiments, conditions cannot be controlled with the same precision and certainty that they can in a laboratory.

Example

Plants usually have natural enemies such as insects and diseases. Lantana camara, commonly referred to as lantana, was introduced to Australia as a garden plant and has since become a widespread bushland weed. In the field, scientists record the abundance of the insects on the lantana plants and the amount of damage inflicted on the bushes.

Try this

A group of scientists carried out research on a rare, ground-dwelling bird, which lives in a national park. The drawings below are of the rare ground-dwelling bird and a similar, common ground-dwelling bird that also lives in the park. The drawings have been reduced to 25% of the actual bird size.

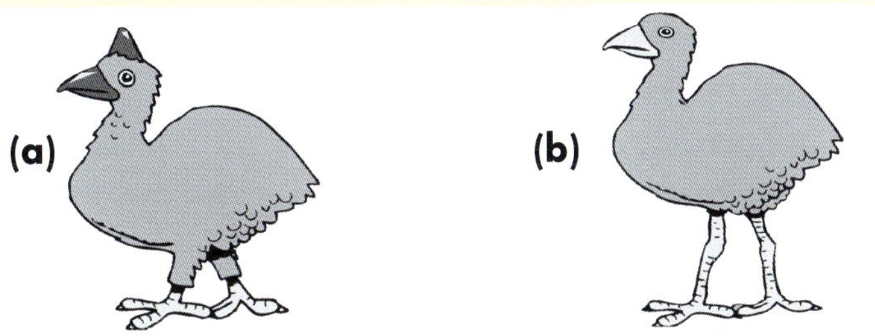

Drawings of the rare (a) and common (b) ground-dwelling birds

The beaks of both these birds have similar appearances but different colours.
The differences have been recorded in the table below.

1 Complete the table by naming and describing two more features that you can see.
2 What is the actual height of the rare ground-dwelling bird?

Feature	Description	Description
	Rare ground bird	**Common ground bird**
Beak	Wide at the base and dark in colour	Wide at the base and light in colour
Head		
Legs		

Study systems

Scientists identify systems and the parts (components) of systems. Components can be dependent on each other or they can interact. A change in one component can affect all the components of a system because of the relationship between the parts.

Example

A system, such as an ecosystem, has boundaries, inputs and outputs. The relationships between the living and non-living parts and their interactions may involve forces operating in opposite directions. But the system as a whole appears to be stable and seems to work together.

The idea of a system allows us to analyse a complex situation by looking at it in terms of inputs, outputs and processes. Is the human body a system?

Compare things

Scientists are constantly comparing things in their search for similarities and differences. Taxonomists are scientists who look for these patterns so that they can identify, describe and name things. By grouping things which are similar, scientists can better understand the relationships between objects, between living organisms, and between living and non-living things.

Example

By working out the similarities and differences between organisms and materials in the natural world, scientists are able to explain the features of a tiger, an apple or a rock.

Try this

List the differences between these two fish.

Name things

When a life form is classified, biologists describe it and give it a scientific name. This name identifies it and shows which group it belongs to in the living world. Names are often based on the unique characteristics of the life form or where it grows. Scientists have agreed to use Latin as the international language for naming living things. The name given to a living thing is a binomial name, which consists of a genus name followed by a species name.

Carolus Linnaeus worked out this binomial classification system for living things

Example

The earliest flower fossil ever discovered originated underwater and was found in China.

Scientists called it Archaefructus sinensis, which means 'ancient fruit from China'.

Scientists create names all the time. For example, a large, red ant that is only found in Australia could be called the 'Australian Red Ant'. This would be the ant's common name.

Invent a binomial name for this animal.

(Clue: Latin words that may help are *macro* meaning large, *rubens* meaning red, *australis* meaning Australian)

Try this

Test ideas

Scientists put their observations to the test in experiments that refine and evolve new theories. A lot of science is trial and error. You try something and it does not work, so you adapt or change the set-up and then you try again, and so on. A **fair test** is an investigation where one variable is changed and all other conditions are kept the same.

Collaborate

In modern times, teams of scientists, engineers, researchers and technicians – rather than a lone inventor – often work together to systematically investigate a problem. Scientists co-operate with one another in order to come up with the best solution.

Try this

Example

Thomas Edison invented the first practical light bulb but it was his modern industrial research laboratory combined with teamwork that developed the first complete electrical distribution system and installed the world's first central electric-light power plant in New York City.

Today making surfboards is a multi-million dollar business. Read the information below and match the specialists to their knowledge/skills contribution by matching the number with the correct letter.

Specialist	Knowledge/skills contribution
1 Designers of F18 fighter planes	**A** Knowledge of how fluids move
2 Visionaries like Ben Lexon who designed the winged keel for sailing boats	**B** Developed rough Teflon finishes (Gorilla Grip) from shark skin
3 Technicians who can design systems that control things	**C** Knowledge of skilful marketing and finance
4 Business experts	**D** Imaginative design work
5 Scientists specialising in water flow	**E** Understanding machinery
6 Scientists specialising in surfaces	**F** Knowledge of designs that move very fast
7 Manufacturers who can use machines to create products	**G** Skills in experimenting and testing
8 Technologists who can develop new ways to do things	**H** Developed wetsuits and leg ropes

Communicate

Scientists learn from each other. They discuss their findings with each other so that their ideas can build on other's ideas. Sharing knowledge is a behaviour that is taken for granted but it is a very special and important behaviour for scientists. Research publishing is used by researchers to make their work available for a wider audience. Most research works are published as journal articles. These publications are accepted as valid contributions to human understanding.

Use technology

Scientists use research knowledge, animations, models, simulations and communication technologies to share information and to extend the boundaries of the laboratory. A model is a simplified imitation of an object, a situation or an idea that helps to make difficult scientific concepts clearer.

Example

British scientist, Francis Crick, as a child, said worriedly to his mother, 'By the time I grow up everything will have been discovered'. In 1953, American scientist, James Watson and Francis Crick developed the model for deoxyribonucleic acid (DNA). This chemical had been deduced to be the carrier of inheritance. This model supported understanding of how genes work.

Models of helicopters were designed 400 years ago but none were built until quite recently. What technology had to be invented before a helicopter could be successfully built and used? Hint: it gives the helicopter its power to run.

Make decisions

Scientific research is influenced by the needs of society. The application of science to our lives allows us to make informed decisions about issues at all levels. Scientists consider the ethical applications of science. They evaluate claims so that they can make reasoned judgements about social, environmental and personal issues. Scientists do this before engaging in scientific decision making.

Example

Which diseases should receive research funding? Should the population of a living thing be controlled? Questions such as these are decided by considering how the decision affects others, the environment and other living organisms.

Try this

Scientific and medical researchers routinely use animals in experiments. For each product listed below, should we use animals in the research?

1 A drug to reverse diabetes
2 A new dishwashing detergent that leaves the user's hands soft and moisturised
3 A cure for cancer
4 A sunscreen that provides a higher level of protection

THE QUALITIES OF A SCIENTIST

Where would we be if Einstein did not have a thirst for knowledge and a respect for reason?

Creativity

Scientists think broadly and deeply and they are flexible and open minded. They do everything with a creative twist. Creativity tends to work away inside your mind and then unexpectedly pops out of your subconscious when you least expect it. It also tends to disappear just when you most need it!

Example
Einstein, Newton and Da Vinci had the knack with lateral thinking. They would allow their mind to wander over, under and around the problem without making any real effort to find the solution. Then they would suddenly just 'see' the solution.

A woman has no map and is walking along a track in a strange country. She comes to an intersection where the signpost has been knocked down. There is no one to ask for directions. How will she know which way to head? Use your creative thinking skills to solve this problem.

Try this

Honesty and integrity

Scientists have an attitude of openness and responsibility when conducting an experiment. Detailed record keeping is essential. It provides evidence of the effectiveness of the procedure used. Accurate record keeping also assists in reproducing the experimental results.

Scepticism

Scientists are confident when conversing about science. Scientists do not just accept information, they are sceptical and question claims about scientific matters.

Imagination

A good imagination is a real asset for a scientist. Intuition and inspiration are part of the systematic procedure called the 'scientific process'. It is this process that scientists use to find answers.

'To raise new questions and new possibilities, to regard old problems from a new angle, requires creative imagination and marks real advances in science'
Einstein

Example

When news of Alexander Graham Bell's new invention, the telephone, reached Britain's chief engineer, he replied: 'The Americans have need of the telephone, but we do not. We have plenty of messenger boys.'
This statement is an example of a 'total failure of imagination'.

At the end of the nineteenth century, carriage builders of the time refused to believe that the invention of the motor car would have any impact at all on the horse and carriage trade.
What effect would this serious lack of imagination have on the carriage builder?

Try this

Ethics

Scientists act with moral integrity and regard for others. They possess a desire and capacity to work for the common good. They apply ethical guidelines in the gathering of evidence.

The ethics of science is also concerned with the possible harmful effects of applying the results of scientific research.

Example

Scientific discoveries are not always put to good use. Nuclear energy made nuclear war possible. In 1945, an atomic bomb was dropped on the Japanese city of Hiroshima. It destroyed the city, 80 000 people died and many more were affected by radiation sickness.

In the future, the living cells of unborn human babies may keep other people alive, healthy and youthful. Under what circumstances would you accept the use of the cells of an unborn foetus?

Wisdom

Science is able to tell us what **can** be done but we have to also consider what **ought** to be done. Science used wisely can make the world a better place; science used unwisely can be a disaster.

Example

Organ transplants, now relatively common, improve the quality of life for many people.
Meat meal is made from the offal (organs) of cattle. In the United Kingdom, the feeding of meat meal to cattle as feed resulted in Mad Cow Disease. Many animals and people died from the disease.
Decisions should be based not on media spin but on valid scientific evidence. It is also important to consider the consequences of your choices.

Try this

Scientists share attitudes and ways of thinking that are relevant to the natural world. They also share attitudes about what can be learned about the world. The table below lists ten attitudes that scientists possess. Match the attitude with how it relates to the scientific enterprise.

Scientific attitude	Relates to the scientific enterprise
Thirsty for understanding and knowledge	**A** There is no absolute certainty in knowledge
Relying on data	**B** Seeing new possibilities in the data
Willingness to modify explanations	**C** Valuing patterns of thought that lead from data to conclusions and eventually to the construction of theories
Respecting reason	**D** Nature's relationships are sometimes best revealed by patterns and formulas
Being honest	**E** Viewing information objectively and without bias
Understanding that all knowledge has tolerance limits	**F** Scientists are addicted to puzzles
Respect for mathematics as a language of science	**G** Explaining natural occurrences by collecting and ordering information, testing ideas, and respecting the information that is revealed

SCIENCE IN SOCIETY

Intercultural understanding

All types of people from wide ranging cultures, over many centuries, have contributed to the accumulation of our scientific knowledge. Science values and recognises the similarities and differences between cultures. Science creates connections between countries and cultivates respect between people. People from many countries have contributed to the advancement of science.

For example, Australia's aboriginals have always applied their understanding of the natural sciences to meet their needs. The countries of the Asian region are in collaboration in addressing global challenges such as climate change, biodiversity, and genetic engineering.

Current issues

The biosphere is a dynamic system providing conditions that sustain life on Earth. Human activity impacts on the sustainability of the biosphere.

Scientists today are wondering about issues such as global warming, possible life on a meteorite, cancer risk from stem cells, dark matter, sustainability, superconductivity and avian flu.

Example

Sustainability is the ongoing capacity of the Earth to maintain life. It aims to reduce our ecological footprint and support quality of life. Sustainable patterns of living meet the needs of the present without compromising the ability of future generations to meet their needs.

Try this

Population growth threatens the environment and our ability to live sustainably. Australia's population growth rate is one of the highest in the developed world. However, Australia has a very low population density (the amount of people that can be sustained by this country). Much of the continent is considered unable to support the densities found in well watered, fertile regions of the world.

What do you think is the best population for Australia? Is it more or less than the 22 million that we now have?

GLOSSARY

abiotic – Non-living things in an ecosystem
absorb – When something 'soaks up' energy instead of reflecting it or letting it pass through
acceleration – The rate of change of velocity
acid rain – Rain that has been made acidic by atmospheric pollutants
adaptation – A feature or a behaviour that helps a living thing to survive
air resistance – The friction force on something moving through the air (drag)
algae – A group of simple plant-like organisms that make their own food by photosynthesis
amplitude – The size of the vibrations that produce sound and determine loudness
analyse – To consider in detail for the purpose of finding meaning or relationships
angiosperms – Plants that reproduce by growing flowers
asexual reproduction – Reproduction involving only one parent and the young have the same characteristics as the parent
assumptions – The differences between what is observed and what is taken for granted
asteroid – A small, rocky object revolving around the Sun
atom – The smallest unit of a chemical element, which contain electrons, protons and neutrons
attract – To pull together by a force as in a magnetic force
axis – Imaginary line drawn through the poles of the Earth around which it spins
battery – Provides the energy to continually separate electrons from protons and push the electrons along a wire
binomial name – Two-part scientific name given to a living thing
biodegradable – A substance that can be broken down by natural processes
biodiversity – The variety of species in an area
biomass – The sum of the mass of all the individual species in an ecosystem
biosphere – Every region of the Earth that is inhabited by living things
biotic – Living things in an ecosystem
cells – The basic building blocks of living things
centre of gravity – The point around which all the atoms (or weight) of an object are centred
chemical reaction – An irreversible process where the chemical form of a substance is changed
chlorophyll – Pigment in plant used for photosynthesis
chloroplast – Elements in plant cells that allow the plant to capture the energy from the sun and make its own food
circuit – A continuous pathway through which electrons (current) flow
climate – This is the average weather conditions of a particular place
clone – Genetically identical individuals or cells
combustion – The chemical change producing heat, in which oxygen reacts with another substance
comet – A small body of ice and dust that orbits the Sun
community – A collection of living things that are found in the same area
compound – This is a pure substance made up of more than one kind of atom
concave – A mirror or lens that curves in like a cave
conclusion – A judgement based on evidence
condenses – The turning of invisible water vapour into water drops and ice
conduction – The process whereby heat is transferred from particle to particle in a solid
conductor – A substance that energy can pass through

constant – Something that does not change
constant velocity – An object moving in a certain direction at a constant speed
continuous data – Any value within a certain range
controlled variable – A variable that is kept constant during an investigation
convection – Process that occurs when heat is transferred in liquids and gases by moving particles
convex – A mirror or lens that curves outwards
core – Hot metallic centre of the Earth which is thought to be solid on the inside and liquid on the outside
craters – Indentations in the surface of planets and moons formed by the impact of meteorites
crust – The Earth's solid, outermost layer (up to 70 km thick) on which we live
crystal – Forms when the molecules of a material are all the same shape and fit together in a clear, many-sided package with flat sides – for example salt, emeralds and sapphires
data – Information that is recorded
death – When the conditions for living stop and the organism's cells break down
decibel – The unit of measure for the loudness of sound, usually measured with a sound meter
deforestation – The permanent removal of trees from the landscape
dense – Tightly packed atoms of a substance
density – The mass or number of atoms or molecules in a certain volume
dependent variable – A variable that changes in response to changes to the independent variable
design – Plan of an investigation
diet – The type of food an animal eats
discrete data – A certain value
drag – Resistance of movement between solids, liquids and gases
earthquake – A series of waves in the Earth, which start where stress along a fault exceeds the elastic limit of the rock so that sudden movement occurs along the edge of the plate
eclipse – The shadow of a celestial body
ectotherm – Cold-blooded animal
electric current – Flow of electricity
electricity – Flow of electrons
electrodes – Metal connectors on a battery
electrons – Negatively charged particles in an atom
element – A pure substance which cannot be decomposed into simpler substances
emulsion – A mixture of liquids where one of the liquids exists as tiny droplets evenly spaced throughout the other liquid
endotherm – Warm-blooded animal
environment – Living and non-living surroundings
erosion – Movement of rock fragments by glaciers, wind, running water and waves
eutrophication – The increase in the nutrient content of a body of water, leading to a rapid increase in algae growth and a decrease in the oxygen level in the water, until it cannot support other aquatic life forms
evaluating – Making judgements and offering opinions
evaporation – The loss of water from the Earth's surface as water vapour
evidence – Data that is considered reliable and valid and can be used to support a particular idea, conclusion or decision
evolution – The process of growth or development
feeding – The process of taking in food
fertilisation – The stage in sexual reproduction when male and female sex cells join together to form a single cell
food chain – A food pathway that connects one species in an ecosystem with another
food web – A collection of food chains
force – Something that changes the shape or motion of an object

frequency – The number of vibrations per second or the number of sound waves that pass a particular point in a given time
friction – The force that resists movement when one surface slides against another
galaxy – A collection of billions of stars and matter held together by gravity
gas – A substance that has no fixed volume, but does take up the volume of its container
genotype – The genetic make-up of an individual
geological time – A timetable of the Earth's history
germination – When a seed starts to develop into a plant
global warming – An increase in the Earth's average temperature due to deforestation and the burning of fossil fuels
gravity – The invisible force of attraction between any two objects
greenhouse effect – The trapping of heat by the Earth's atmosphere
gymnosperms – A plant with seeds that develop without a protective covering (naked seeds)
habitat – The living place of a species
hertz (Hz) – Unit for frequency which is the number of vibrations per second
homeostasis – The maintenance of a range of conditions within which an organism can function
hypothesis – An idea based on observation that can be supported or proved false by experiment
independent variable – The variable that is changed in an investigation to see what effect it has on the dependent variable
inertia – An object's resistance to change in motion, depending on its mass
insulation – Trapping air to stop heat being released
insulator – A substance that will not let energy pass through it
interpreting – Explaining the meaning of an experience or data
investigation – The scientific process of answering a question or solving a problem
joules – Unit of measure for energy
kinetic energy – Energy of a moving object
life cycle – A predictable pattern of change that an organism goes through in its life
light year – The distance that light travels in one year
liquid – A substance that maintains its volume but takes the shape of the container
literature search – Reviewing available information or data that supports the proposed research
living organism – Anything that has the characteristics of respiration, excretion, nutrition, growing and developing, sensitivity to the surrounding world and the ability to reproduce
magma – Hot molten rock under the Earth's surface
magnetic field – This is the area around a magnet where it attracts or repels
mantle – The layer of the Earth's interior between the crust and the core
mass (biology) – A measure of how much matter in an object (how many atoms), measured in grams (g) or kilograms (kg)
mass (physics) – Amount of matter in a substance
matter – Groups of molecules
metabolism – All the chemical processes that take place in a living thing
meteor – A piece of dust which burns up as it enters the Earth's atmosphere
meteorite – A chunk of rock or metal from space, too big to burn up and which lands on Earth
Milky Way – A band of stars: the visible portion of the spiralling, disk-shaped galaxy in which our solar system is located
mixture – Made up of two or more substances (either elements or compounds) which are not chemically combined and not in definite proportions
model – A representation that describes, simplifies or clarifies the workings, structure or relationships within an object, system or idea

molecule – The smallest part of an element or compound able to exist independently
newton –The unit that we use to measure forces
niche – The role of a living thing in its environment
nuclear fission – Splits large atoms into smaller atoms, releasing enormous amounts of energy
nuclear fusion – A nuclear reaction that releases large amounts of energy when larger atoms form smaller ones
nucleus (biology) – A cell's control centre which contains the organism's genetic information
nucleus (physics) – The dense central core of an atom consisting of protons and neutrons
observing – Hearing, seeing or touching something
opaque – A material that does not let light through
ozone – A colourless gas whose molecules are made up of three oxygen atoms joined together and it forms a layer that keeps out most of the Sun's damaging ultraviolet rays
pattern – Repeated occurrences or sequences
Periodic Table of Elements – An arrangement of the known elements
phases of the moon – The lunar cycle moves from the new moon phase where it is completely invisible, to full moon (waxing) and back to new moon again (waning)
phenomenon – Something that impresses the observer
phloem – A tissue that carries nutrients throughout a plant
physical change – A reversible change in the state (solid, liquid, gas) or appearance of a substance
pitch – How high or low a sound is
planet – A large body held in orbit about a star by gravity, which shines only by reflected light
pole – Where the magnetic force is strongest in a magnet
pollution – The disruption of the natural world by the release of chemicals or other agents
potential energy – Energy stored in an object because of its position or because of its condition
prediction – A specific forecast about a future event based on a tested and accepted hypothesis
properties – The characteristics which help distinguish a substance from all other substances
proton – The large, positively charged particles in the nucleus of an atom
pure substance – A substance that has a constant chemical composition
radiation – The spread of electromagnetic radiation and other sub-atomic particles
radioactive – The emission of alpha, beta and gamma rays from the break-up of certain nuclei
reflection – Light or sound bouncing off whatever it strikes
reflects – When light or sound bounces off a surface
refraction – The change of direction of a ray of light in passing from one substance to another
reliability – The extent to which repeated observations or data, taken under identical circumstances, will produce similar results
repel – To push away using a force
reproduction – The production of offspring
research – To locate, gather, record and analyse information in order to develop understanding
resultant force – The force produced when two like forces are added
salinity – The concentration of salts in the root zone of a plant by evaporation from a shallow water table
satellite – An object that orbits a planet
science – What scientists use to answer the questions
scientific investigation – The response to a question or a problem

scientific method – An activity which involves the testing of a prediction or hypothesis resulting in the drawing of a conclusion about the question or problem
sedimentary rocks – Rocks which form when small pieces of rocks are worn off and then washed into low places where they gather in layers
shivering – The repeated contraction of surface muscles to produce heat
Solar System – The planets, asteroids, comets, and other bodies that orbit the Sun
solid – Something that maintains its shape
solution – A mixture where the molecules of a solid (the solute) are completely intermingled with the molecules of a liquid (the solvent)
stomata – Slits in the outer layer of leaves
subduction – Subsidence of the leading edge of a plate into the mantle
Sun – The star in the centre of the Solar System
suspension – A mixture where an insoluble solid is suspended in a liquid
sweating – The secretion of moisture from the skin to cool the body
switch – A bridge for electrons, which can be lifted out of the circuit so the electrons can no longer flow
terminals – The connections on a battery to allow the flow of energy
thermoregulation – The control and adjustment of body temperature
translucent – This is a material that transmits some light but is not transparent such as frosted glass
transparent – This is a material that lets light through such as glass
trophic level – The position of a species in a food chain
tsunamis – Gigantic destructive waves mostly caused by an underwater earthquake
variable – A factor that can be changed, kept the same or measured in an investigation
vasodilation – A widening of blood vessels
vector quantity – This is a quantity that has direction such as velocity
velocity – Speed in a particular direction
vibrations – To-and-fro movements that produce sounds
volcano – An opening – like a safety valve – in the Earth's crust through which magma, gases, solid rock fragments, poisonous fumes and ash can be discharged
wavelength – The distance from the crest of one sound wave to the crest of another
weather – The term used to describe atmospheric conditions in a specific place at a specific time
weight – The force of gravity that pulls an object towards the Earth
xylem – A plant tissue that carries water and minerals from the soil to the leaves
zygote – A fertilised egg

Try this ANSWERS

SCIENCE INQUIRY SKILLS

Page 12 Senses
Eye (D), nose (E), tongue (A), ear (C), skin (B)

Page 13 Is observing seeing?
1 Tree with seedlings growing under it
2 Seedlings mostly on one side of tree
3 More nutrients and sunlight or the wind blew

Page 13 Measuring
B in both cases

Page 14 Hypothesis
E, A, D, F, C, B

Page 15 Recipe for hypothesis
1 Sunburn will be the result
2 Does wearing a t-shirt protect you from UV radiation when you are swimming?
3 'Wearing a t-shirt protects you from UV radiation whilst you are swimming'

Page 16 Hypothesis formulation
1 Yes
2 No – this is a question
3 Yes
4 No – more than one variable
5 No – not specific enough
6 No – too big to get one simple answer
7 Yes

Page 17 Predictions from a hypothesis
1 Light will not go on
2 Bulb has blown
3 Replace bulb with a new one
4 When bulb is replaced, the light will work
5 Modify your hypothesis and then test new one

Page 18 What is a variable?
1 Must be all milk chocolate and sample to be tested must be the same size
2 Quality of the chocolate
3 Different groups of people have different preferences – age, sex, ethnic background
4 We could rate each chocolate from 1→4

Page 19 Types of variables
Independent variable – water temperature
Dependant variable – dissolving speed
Controlled variables – amount of salt, type of salt, rate of stirring

Page 21 Checklist for experimental design
1 Place the filter papers in the containers
2 Label four containers with the salt solution and one 'control'
3 Add water to control and other four containers so paper is moist
4 Sprinkle a set number of seeds onto the wet paper in all containers
5 Cover with plastic wrap to stop the paper drying
6 Place all containers in the same position
7 Observe what happens over the next two weeks

Page 22 Characteristics of good experimental design
1 (D) – P and Q each need to be tested on a large group of bald subjects and the results compared to a control group of untreated bald subjects
2 Yes – large groups in both the control and experimental group
3 Yes – all relevant variables had a control
4 To ensure there are no mistakes in the experimental design

Page 23 Laboratory apparatus
1 24 millimetres
2 20 degrees Celsius
3 55 millilitres

Page 25 Recording measurements
No table title
Independent and dependant variables in wrong column
Heading for each column is not detailed enough
No units supplied

Page 26 Data handling skills
1 How light refracts
2 The white light source
3 Red
4 Diagram

Page 27 Discrete or continuous data
1 Continuous
2 Discrete
3 Discrete
4 Continuous
5 Discrete

Page 29 Appropriate graph format
Histogram
Pie graph

Page 31 Rules for drawing a graph
1 Fish caught in a trawler net
2 Length of fish
3 Centimetres
4 Number of fish caught
5 There were no fish less than 1cm long
6 50%

Page 32 Data analysis and evaluation
E
Z, X and Y
Repeated pattern is XYYYXZXYZ

Page 34 Checklist for evaluating evidence
1 a. 6; b. glass; c. air/plastic sandwich; d. 31 minutes; e. 3 minutes
2 Glass, nylon, leather, air/plastic sandwich, aluminium, polystyrene
3 Air/plastic sandwich
4 It is expanded plastic so also contains air
5 Set up several cans in each insulator and average the results for each. Repeat the whole experiment several times
6 Better control of variables – same thickness

of the containers, same space between the container and the can, the exact starting temperature of each can.
Check that temperature was read accurately and consistently.

7 Suggestions – use other materials for the containers, test the insulators for use in an esky, keep other types of drinks cold, more detailed work on heat transfer in materials

Page 36 Conclusion

The conclusion is: 'The snatch strap extension is related to the load until it reaches its elastic limit. The two variables are related and the hypothesis has been supported'.

Page 37 Writing a report in scientific format

Title	Bicycle speeds over different terrain
Intro	The speed of a bicycle over different terrain helps when planning for a race.
Review of literature	Bicycle speeds vary with the terrain.
Aim/ hypothesis	Bicycle speed will decrease going up the hill.
Method/ equipment	Start the bicycle at the bottom of the hill Record speed at time 0, 2min, 4min, 6min, 8min, 10min. Stopwatch, person riding a bicycle, a suitable hill
Discussion	The bicycle lost speed on upward slopes, was steady on flat ground and gained speed on the downward slopes. This investigation needs to be repeated several times, with all the variables controlled before we can have faith in the results. Human error in using the stopwatch should also be minimised.
Conclusion	The cyclist lost speed going up the hill and gained it going down and was fairly constant across the top. The hypothesis was supported.

Page 38 Checklist for report writing

The research team were interested in what plant species were growing where the pH of the soil had been increased by alkaline runoff from a building site. The equipment required is listed below. The following data was recorded – exact location of each section, the plant species and the pH in each section. After analysing the data, the team concluded that the high pH levels stopped the growth of only some plants.

BIOLOGICAL SCIENCES

Page 39 The condition of being alive

We take it from the tree and eat it or cook it.

Page 40 Dorsal and ventral – fins; anterior – head; posterior – tail; lateral – stripe

Page 41 Cells – the basic unit of life

1 Muscle
2 Heart
3 Digestive tract

Page 42 Classification of life

Dad – short lashes, dimples, raise eyebrow; Mum – hair colour

Page 43 Plants – B, D; animals living in water – G; animals that do not live in water – A, C, E, F, H, I; animals with bones – A, C, E, H, I; animals without bones – F, G

Page 44 1 Monotreme
2 Echidna
3 Electro sensors
4 Electro sensors

Page 45 Plant groups

1 Pine trees, palm trees, fruit trees, lettuce
2 Timber

Page 46 Plant structures

A. bud, B. flower, C. leaf, D. stem, E. root

Page 48 Plant processes

'C' because the stomata, through which water is lost, are on the lower surface of leaves

Page 48 Plant growth

Germination was not a problem. But as soon as they began to grow, they grew around and around, totally confused about where to send their shoots and roots. There was no gravity to give them directions.

Page 49 Plant reproduction

The bee transports these male cells or pollen to the pistil of another flower. These male cells fertilise the female cells in the ovary and seeds then develop.

Page 51 Animal groups

1 Insects and higher plants
2 69 000 divided by total species (1 413 000) = about 5%

Page 52 Animal systems

Nerves (nervous system) send a message from the hand to the brain, the brain processes the information and sends a message back to the muscles (muscular system) of the hand, the muscles move the bones (skeletal system) in the hand and the hand is moved

Page 53 Animal processes

All cases maximise the use of air as an insulator by trapping it and preventing body heat from escaping

Page 54 Animal growth

Strong jaws, large head, camouflage, warning colours, stinging hairs

Page 55 Animal feeding

Herbivore – grinding teeth, bacterial digestive stomach with four parts
Carnivore – teeth that cut and tear, strong jaws for ripping
Omnivore – teeth for grinding as well as tearing
Detritus feeders – have strong appendages for gripping and tearing
Filter feeders – a structure that sieves food from water: baleen plates, fine tentacles

Page 56 Animal senses

Animal	dingo	bat	owl	eagle
Sense	smell, hearing, sight	sound (echoes)	hearing, sight)	sight

Page 57 Animal communication
1 Bee 1
2 More than 100 metres away and slightly to the left of the sun

Page 59 Animal behaviour
1 Sperm whale
2 Kangaroo
3 Cougar
4 Cheetah

Page 60 Animal reproduction
Asexual – 2, 7, 8; sexual – 1, 3, 4, 5, 6

Page 62 Environment
1 Pond (freshwater muscle – filters food from the water, water beetle – plant eater, water spider – meat eater)
2 Lawn (lawn grub –plant eater, land spider – meat eater)
3 Flower bed (earthworm: eats dead animals and plants, lizard: eats meat, caterpillar: eats plants)

Page 63 Flow of energy and matter in the natural world
Pyramid B

Page 65 1 Tree
2 Six
3 Six (mistletoe, tree, insects, mice, birds, fox)
4 Carnivores (mice, birds, eagle, fox), herbivores (rabbits, possums, insects)

Page 66 A, E, D, C, F, B

Page 66 Survival and the interaction of living things
1 There would be more insects and therefore more birds, more eagles and foxes
2 There would be a lot less insects, more birds, more eagles and foxes. However, the insects would eventually run out, the mice would mostly die, many of the birds, eagles and foxes would die, so much so that the ecosystem may become unbalanced.

Page 67 A. Hard seed coat; B. holes and spines on leaves;
C. insulation; D. perfume and a white colour;
E. water storage and spines

Page 68 Ecosystem balance
Many will die in the process and since the entire habitat is destroyed, there will be no food or shelter for animals

Page 69

Food chain	tiny plants	tiny animals	fish	heron
Pesticide (ppm)	0.02	10	200	1600

PHYSICAL SCIENCES

Page 71 How does energy behave?
1 Energy can be transferred from one object to another. You give the first coin in the row energy by pushing it. The energy passes through all the coins until it reaches the last coin in the row. There is no coin in front of this coin to prevent it from moving, so it shoots forward with about the same energy that you gave the first coin.
2 Two coins supply enough energy to shoot two coins out

Page 73 Kinetic energy
Your lungs are working as machines, forcing air into the balloon. Energy is stored in the springiness of squashed air inside the elastic balloon and in the elastic material of the balloon. When the balloon bursts all the stored (potential) energy becomes a blast of air – an explosion, which carries the confetti around the room.

Page 75 Heat transfer
A. convection; B. conduction; C. radiation

Page 75 Conductors and insulators
The paper clip on the copper rod will fall off first as heat is conducted best in copper. Heat is conducted very poorly in aluminium and not at all in glass.

Page 76 Controlling heat transfer
A. It melts; B. it melts faster; C. Not enough energy was transmitted through the outside layer of meringue to melt the ice-cream at the centre. The sponge cake and the meringue contain lots of air bubbles and so are good insulators.

Page 76 Expansion and contraction
1 Bridges are often made of steel bars, which expand in the heat and contract in the cold. The gaps are to prevent crumpling and stretching
2 If they were tight, then in winter when they contract they will pull the poles out or snap the wires
3 The liquid inside expands providing a measure of how hot or cold something is

Page 77 What is light?
No, because light travels in straight lines and cannot go around corners

Page 78 What colour is light?
An object absorbs only its own colour and reflects all the rest, so green is the only colour reflected

Page 79 Sensing light
No, a beam of light by itself cannot be seen. The beam is only visible if there is dust, smoke or fog in the air for the light to bounce off.

Page 80 Reflection – bouncing light
The water droplets on the surface of the mirror would reflect the light back in many directions, resulting in a blurred image

Page 81 Refraction – bending light
Light rays bend when they pass from one substance to another, this is called refraction

Page 82 How we use light
1 The Earth's atmosphere breaks up the white light as it bounces off air molecules. When the sun is directly overhead in the middle of the day, blue light is scattered the most and so the sky looks blue.
2 The moon does not have an atmosphere so light cannot be scattered and the view is the blackness of never ending nothing (space)
3 Different atmospheres result in different colours – the Martian sky would be pink
4 Blue light is scattered out of the sun's rays so the sun looks yellow

Page 83 What is sound?
Air brakes on trucks

Page 84 Sensing sound
Rabbit; no

Page 84 How sound travels
Sound cannot travel through a vacuum or through space because there are no molecules to pass on the energy vibrations

Page 86 Musical sounds
Missing words in order: size; loudness; small; soft; frequency; pitch; vibrations; low; high; high; amplifiers

Page 87 Sound and our world
1340 metres (4 x 330) – lightening is light and travels faster than sound waves

Page 89 Types of electricity
1 The bulb lights up
2 No – string is an insulator
3 Put a gap in the circuit so the electrons cannot get right around it

Page 90 Building circuits
1 In Circuit A only bulb (1) comes on, in Circuit B both bulbs come on
2 Circuit B

Page 92 Balanced and unbalanced forces
1 Lift (upward force), thrust (forward push), gravity (weight) and drag (air resistance = friction caused by air rubbing against the plane as it moves)
2 Lift and thrust must be stronger than gravity and drag
3 Lift must equal the pull of gravity and thrust must be stronger than the drag of resistance.

Page 94 Contact forces
1 Increase, greater, gravity, slows down
2 An open parachute drops slowly because it traps air under it, which pushes upwards (air resistance) and slows the speed of the fall. This upwards force works against gravity.
3 If an object is lifted above the Earth it has gravitational potential energy, if this force is less than gravity, gravity will win and the object falls.

Page 95 Non-contact forces
1 The yo-yo would not fall but could be flipped to the end of the string and then would behave fairly normally
2 Yes, but not as good as with gravity
3 This is called geotrophism – roots grow towards gravity and shoots grow away from gravity
4 The mouse does not have enough mass for gravity to be a danger. However, a rat would be killed

Page 96 The magnetic field flows out of the north pole and back to the south pole. The north pole of one magnet attracts the south pole of another. Like poles repel, therefore, the magnets separate.

Page 97 Newton's first law of motion
The car has stopped but the man's inertia tries to keep him moving at the same speed and in the same direction

Page 98 Newton's second law of motion
Yes

Page 99 F= ma, F = 1 x 9.8 = 9.8N

Page 99 Newton's third law of motion
The force of the gases rushing in one direction (action) sends the rocket in the opposite direction (reaction)

CHEMICAL SCIENCES

Page 100 What is matter?
1 No, everything in the Universe is either matter, energy or the space between the atoms that make up the matter
2 107 different atoms or elements
3 Wood, paper, paddle pop sticks and even you are 18% carbon
4 Soft drink cans, aluminium foil
5 This material is called water

Page 101 Characteristics of matter
1 They both weigh the same
2 Butter because it has more mass (more atoms in the same space)
3 A light rock has less molecules and therefore takes less energy to move it

Page 103 Mixtures
1 Solution (solid + liquid + gas)
2 Gas

Page 103 Pure substances
Elements – silver pendant, aluminium foil
Compounds – polythene wrapping film
Mixtures – confetti, fruit cake

Page 104 The 'states of matter'
1 It becomes a gas (water vapour)
2 It becomes a liquid again (water)
3 It becomes a solid (ice)
4 This process can be reversed by just adding energy.

Page 105 Solids, liquids and gases
1 Water definitely has holes in it but they are very small – the molecules slide around and allow you to walk or swim through them
2 The atoms are far too close together in a solid to permit you to run through
3 A gas is easy to run through as there is lots of space – the atoms are far apart
4 No, because objects could move through it and it would eventually float away

Page 106 Combining the states of matter
1 The ice-cream stabilises the bubbles in the soda to hold the bubbles in place for longer
2 Shaving cream, expanded polystyrene (esky)

Page 107 Physical change
Put chocolate into the fridge, evaporate the water from the tea, remould the chalk dust, heat and remould the nylon threads

Page 107 It is designed to pop out when the water in the milk freezes and forms its crystal – the bottle does not crack or burst.

Page 108 Chemical change
1 B
2 Corrosion or rusting
3 Oxygen
4 To stop air getting into the boiled water

Page 109 Properties of materials
1 Fabric, paper, soft plastic sheeting
2 Chalk is brittle and snaps easily, it is not strong, absorbs water and is inflexible which make it unsuitable for construction

Page 110 Natural materials
Bones, spider web, bat wings, trees, honeycomb

Page 110 Processed materials
1 Shrinking is one of the properties of plastics
2 Used to heat seal everything from board games to tooth brushes

Page 111 Strength of materials
The paper was folded to make it thicker, triangle shapes and cylindrical are always stronger.
The attachment of the handle to the rest of the bag: make the handle as part of the bag and reinforce it with masking tape

Page 112 1 Marshmallow is full of air, it is not very dense, it is squishy and cannot support much weight
2 Toothpicks on the other hand are quite rigid
3 The toothpicks are rigid but there is little support for them when they join the marshmallow together
4 The load would be more spread out and more weight could be supported

Page 113 Processing garbage
The floating plastics can look like food to animals and birds. The plastics clog up their stomachs and they die. Also, they get tangled up in plastic and die: for example, fishing lines and 'six pack' rings.

Page 114 Biodegradable materials
Worth considering the alternatives – all the water used to wash millions of plates every day, the water pollution from all the dishwashing detergents and the energy use of the sewerage plants that process all this waste.

Page 115 Recycling materials
1 Organic – bun, cheese, sauce, fries, soft drink, burger wrapper, the fries bag, the serviettes
2 Biodegradable – same as organic
3 Recycled – the cutlery, drink container
4 Land fill – carry bag, burger container

Page 116 Recycling plastics
1 Polystyrene
2 Density is a measure of how closely packed the plastic molecules are

EARTH AND SPACE SCIENCES

Page 117 Keeping track of time
This is the exact time it takes for the Earth to travel around the Sun

Page 118 Geological time

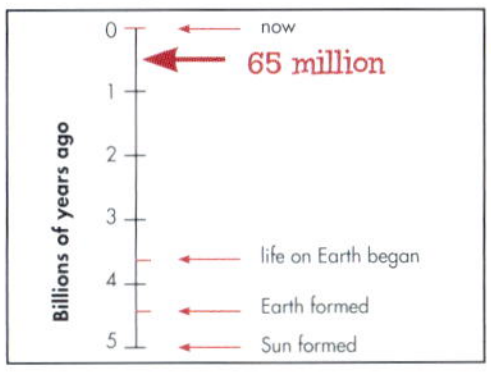

Page 120 Dimensions in time and scale
Jupiter is about 750 million kilometres from Mercury

Page 120 160 000 light years

Page 121 Third rock from the Sun
Gravity

Page 122 Earth's rotations
The Earth would leave it behind

Page 123 The Moon
Earth

Page 124 Planet Earth, Third Rock from the Sun, Solar System, Milky Way, The Universe

Page 125 Structure of the Earth
The crust is thin and solid, but it is not one complete layer. It is made of many shifting tectonic plates that move slowly around, grinding and pushing up against one another.

Page 126 Changing landscapes
Maps; by photographs taken by artificial satellites that orbit the Earth

Page 127 Earth's soils

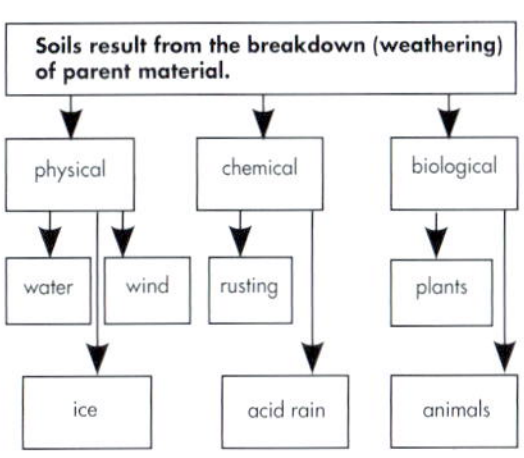

Page 129 Old rock and soil is being returned to the mantle for nutrient renewal by a process called subduction

Page 131 Geo-superstars
The explosion took 1300 feet off the height of the mountain and deposited 3 billion cubic yards of pulverised ice, rock and mud over the surrounding landscape.
The crust would be crumbling and new mountains formed

Page 134 Atmosphere and weather
Wind

Page 134 Clockwise

Page 135 Water and weather
1 Water on the planet is a finite resource
2 We cannot make any more

Page 138 Climate and weather
1 March
2 6 months
3 Low rainfall and sometimes drought

Page 139 Atmosphere and life
Atmosphere, water, soil

Page 140 By raising the level of greenhouse gases, depleting the ozone layer and polluting the atmosphere

Page 141 Water and life
Reduces the transpired water in the atmosphere and so reduces rainfall in the area

Page 142 Eutrofication

Page 143 Soils and life
Primitive man – controlled by the environment
Hunter gatherer – man starts to control the environment
Agriculturalist – man has increased control over the environment
Industrialist – great control over the environment but with many undesirable cons equences

HUMAN ENDEAVOUR

Page 144 Limits of science
No, science knowledge has advanced considerably since then

Page 145 Research
1 Pure
2 Applied
3 Applied
4 Pure

Page 146 Levels of scientific thought
1 Theory
2 No, it is an adage – a common saying that many people consider to be true but is not scientifically valid.

Page 147 Scientific literacy
Points C and F are not valid questions

Page 148 Scientific numeracy
Decibels (dB), newtons, joules (J), 'counts/ minute'

Page 149 Science tips for solving problems
The residual air kept causing the filament to burn; pumped a gas into the bulb instead of trying to remove air; one of the inert gases (helium, neon) as they do not support combustion

Page 150 Observation
1a. and 2b.

Page 150 Visualise
An apple falling from a tree and hitting him on the head

Page 151 Field research
24 centimetres

Feature	Description	Description
Head	Large casque on top of its head.	No casque on top of its head
Legs	Short thick legs	Longer, thinner legs

Page 152 Systems
Yes, we constantly exchange matter with the environment. We take in food and oxygen, process them and then excrete faeces, urine and carbon dioxide.

Page 152 Compare things
Yes –one has an extra dorsal fin and one has a 'V' shaped tail

Page 153 Name things
Perhaps *Macrorubens australis*

Page 154 Collaborate
In order from top to bottom – F, D, G, C, B, A, E, H

Page 155 Use technology
Combustion engine

Page 155 Make decisions
Individual opinion but should provide reasons for opinion.

Page 156 Creativity
Stand the signpost up so the arm indicating the place she has come from is pointing in the same direction. The other arm will then point in the correct direction to head.

Page 157 Imagination
The end of his business

Page 157 Ethics
Individual opinions

Page 158 Wisdom
Top to bottom - F, G, B, C, E, A, D

Page 159 Current issues
Individual response based on accepted scientific views

INDEX

acceleration, 99
acid rain, 140
acoustics, 87
adaptation, 67
algae, 45
amoeba, 40, 43, 54
amphibians, 51
analysing data, 26
anatomists, 40
animals, 50–60
  behaviour, 58
  communication, 57
  diet/food, 54–5, 64
  invertebrates, 50
  life cycle, 53–5
  movement, 56
  processes, 53
  reproduction, 59–60
  senses, 56–7
  systems, 52
  vertebrates, 50–1
angiosperms, 45
arthropods, 50
asexual reproduction, 59
asteroids, 124
atmosphere
  and life, 139–40
  and weather, 133–4
atoms, 100–2
balancing scales, 24
bar graph, 28
bees, 49, 57
biology, 39–69
biodegradable materials, 114
biomagnification, 68
biosphere, 159
birds, 51
butterfly life cycle, 54
carbohydrates, 41
carbon cycle, 66
carnivores, 55
cells, 40–1, 53
chemical energy, 72
chlorophyll, 47, 67
circadian rhythm, 58
circuits, 89–90
circulatory system, 52
climate, 136–8
conifers, 45
classification, 42–4, 153, 154
colours, 78, 81
column graph, 29
comets, 124
communication, 37–8, 57, 86
compounds, 103
computers, 24
conclusion, 35–6
conduction, 74
conductors, 75
convection, 74
Coriolis Effect, 134, 136
Crick, Francis, 155
current electricity, 88
cyclones, 134
data
  discrete and continuous, 27
  evaluation, 32–4
  graphing, 27–31
  measuring and recording, 25
  processing and analysing, 26
decomposer, 64
deforestation, 142
detritus feeders, 55
diffraction gratings, 82
digestive system, 52
dinosaurs, 118
DNA, 41, 155
Earth, 119–24
  crust, 125, 126, 128
  night and day, 122
  poles, 121
  rotation of, 121
  seasons, 122
  structure of, 125–32
  weathering mechanisms, 126–7
earthquakes, 86, 131
echinoderms, 50
echoes, 87
eclipse, 123
ecology, 61–9
ecosystems, 61
  changes in, 97
  cycling of nutrients, 65
  flow of food, 64
  humans and, 68
  life cycles, 66
ectotherm, 53
Edison, Thomas, 154
El Nino Southern Oscillation (ENSO), 137–8
elastic energy, 72
electrical energy, 73, 88–90
elements, 103
endotherm, 53
energy, 70–3
  heat, 74–6
  kinetic, 73
  light, 77–82
  potential, 72
energy flow, 63–5
ENSO *see* El Nino Southern Oscillation
environment, 61–2
environmental disasters, 68–9
equipment, 23–4
ethics, 157

eutrophication, 141
evaluation of data, 32–4
evolution, 67
excretory system, 52
expansion and contraction, 76
experiments
    design, 20–1
    repeatability, 22
    validity, 21
fibre optics, 82
filter feeders, 55
fish, 50
flowering plants, 45, 49
food chains, 63–5
force, 91–6
    balanced and unbalanced, 91
    contact, 91–4
    gravitational, 94
    magnetic, 95
    non-contact, 94–6
friction, 91–2
frog life cycle, 54
Galileo, 98, 117
garbage, 113–16
gases, 104–6
genus, 44
geological time, 118
global warming, 69, 140, 159
graphs, 27–31
gravitational energy, 72
gravity, 92, 94–5, 121
gymnosperms, 45
habitats, 61
    destruction of, 68–9, 142
hazardous waste, 113
hearing, 86
heat energy, 73, 74–6
heat transfer, 74–6
herbivores, 55
histogram, 28
homeostasis, 53
hurricanes, 134
hypothesis, 14–17, 146
insects, 50
instruments, 23–4, 81, 85
insulators, 75
investigation *see* scientific investigation
kinetic energy, 73
La Nina, 137–8
laboratory apparatus, 23–4
landfill, 113–15
Langmuir, Irving, 149
laser, 82
laws, 146
light energy, 73, 77–82
lipids, fats and oils, 41
liquids, 104–6
line graph, 28, 30–1
Linnaeus, Carolus, 153
literature search, 14
magnetic force, 95–6, 121
magnets, 95–6
magnification, 24
mammals, 51
mass, 24
materials, 100
    biodegradable, 114
    chemical changes, 108
    choosing suitable, 111
    classification of, 102–3
    natural, 109–10
    physical changes, 107
    processed, 110
    properties of, 109
    recycling, 114–16
    strength of, 111–12
matter, 100–1
    states of, 104–6
measurement, 13
    recording data, 25
    tools, 24
    units of, 25, 148
metamorphosis, 54
meteors, 124
method *see* scientific method
microscope, 24
migration, 58
Milky Way, 120
minerals, 127
mixtures, 102
molluscs, 50
Moon, 123
motion, 97–9
mountains, 131
muscular system, 52
music, 85
nervous system, 52
Newton, Sir Isaac, 91, 97
Newton's laws of motion, 97–9
niche, 61
night and day, 122
nitrogen cycle, 65
non-flowering plants, 45
nuclear energy, 72, 157
nucleic acids, 41
observation, 12–13
oceans, 136
oil spills, 69
omnivores, 55
optical instruments, 81
organisms, 39
oscilloscope, 85
ozone depletion, 140
packaging, 113, 114
parasite, 64
periscope, 81
personal energy, 72
pesticides, 68
phloem, 46
photosynthesis, 47
pie chart, 28
planets, 119–21
    see also Earth
plants, 45–9
    cells, 41
    flowering, 45, 49
    life cycle, 48

organs, 46
photosynthesis, 47
processes, 47–8
reproduction, 49
structure, 46
transpiration, 47–8
plastic waste, 113
recycling, 115–16
platypus, 44
pollination, 49
pollution, marine, 142
population growth, 159
potential energy, 72
predator, 64
predicting, 12
problem solving, 149
proteins, 41
pure substances, 103
radiation, 74
rainbows, 81
recording data, 25
recycling, 114–16
reflection, 79
refraction, 80
repeatability, 22
reproduction, 59–60
reproductive system, 52
reptiles, 51
research, 144–5, 151, 154
respiratory system, 52
rocks, 127
questioning, 12
salinity, 141
scatter graph, 28
science
current issues, 159
definition, 144
intercultural understanding, 159
limits of, 144
scientific investigation, 11
designing, 20–2
planning, 18–19
report of, 37–8
scientific literacy, 147
scientific method, 11
scientific names, 44
scientific numeracy, 148
scientific report, 37–8
scientific view, 145–8
form and function, 146
order and organisation, 145
patterns, 145
scale and measurement, 146
stability and change, 146
scientists
ethics, 157
role of, 150–5
qualities, 156–8
seasons, 122
seed plants, 45
senses, 12, 56–7
sexual reproduction, 59–60
shadows, 79, 122
skeletal system, 52
skin, 52
soil, 126–9
deforestation, 142
erosion, 142
salinity, 143
solids, 104–6
sonar, 87
sound energy, 73, 83–7
sound waves, 85
Southern Oscillation, 138
space, 119–21, 124
space age, 124
species, 44, 68
stars, 119
static electricity, 88
Sun, 119, 122
sustainability, 159
symbiosis, 64
synchrotron, 82
tectonic plates, 125, 129
temperature, 74
theory, 146
thermal energy *see* heat energy
thermoregulation, 53
thunder, 86
time, 117–18
tools, 23–4
transpiration, 47–8
tsunamis, 132
ultrasound, 87
validity, 21
variables, 18–19
velocity, 98
volcanoes, 130–1
water
and life, 141–2
pollution, 142
water cycle, 135
Watson, James, 155
weather, 133–8
weathering, 126–7
wind, 134
worms, 50
xylem, 46